A Time to Mourn

Judaism and the

Psychology of Bereavement

JACK D. SPIRO

Foreword by Abraham N. Franzblau

BLOCH PUBLISHING COMPANY

New York

New Material Copyright © 1985
Copyright © 1967
By Jack D. Spiro

Library of Congress Catalogue Card Number 67-30744
ISBN: *0-8197-0497-0*

A TIME TO MOURN

Contents

Part I. The Psychological Meaning of Bereavement

Part III. *The Mourning Process in Judaism*

Foreword

Death, the inescapable end of every living creature, is, paradoxically, a fact of life. Rabbi Spiro's excellent book never loses sight of this fact. He keeps us, the living, and the problem which death presents to us, constantly in focus.

As a rabbi, he is naturally concerned with Jewish beliefs and practices, especially the evaluation of their meaning and significance for the modern Jew. He traces those centering around the subject of death in a complete and scholarly manner, treating them in the light of both ancient and modern Jewish tradition.

Then, as a student of psychology, aware of the findings of modern research, he evaluates Jewish mourning rituals and practices against the backdrop of sociology, psychology and psychoanalysis.

The result is a beautiful synthesis—and a fascinating book, affording guide-posts not only for rabbis, but for religious leaders of all faiths, for all religions must deal with the subject of death and must comfort the bereaved. A work like this has never been done before, and has been very much needed.

The subject of death and mourning is not a simple one. It has infinite facets, and has been handled variously by different religions and different cultures in varying times and climes.

Rabbi Spiro considers the dynamics of the process of mourning as it is revealed in modern psychiatric research, but also the Jewish theological background relating to the concept of death, the Hereafter, the soul, bodily resurrection, immortality, superstitions about the ability of the deceased or his "ghost" to influence the survivors or the community, the corpse and its handling, the functionaries involved in the process, burial grounds, and so forth. But all of this is essential to understand the bereaved as mourners, the role of the relatives and of the community at large, and finally, to help in the reintegration of the grief-shattered bereaved into the community of the living, and the restoration of their lives to normalcy.

Rabbi Spiro traces the beliefs and customs through Biblical, Talmudic, medieval, and modern times, enabling us to watch them blossom and ripen into a well-defined culture pattern. At each stage, we are able to see clearly the delicate counterpoint of deep-seated psychological factors which are at play to shape a belief or practice. We see the primitive in its origins and native habitat, and the residuals of it which remain extant today. At the same time, Rabbi Spiro demonstrates the amazingly profound insights which our forefathers displayed, paralleled only by those of the geniuses of our own day.

Freud published his classical paper on "Mourning and Melancholia" in 1917. Subsequently, the subject has been illuminated by his disciples as well as by later writers in and out of the psychoanalytic field. Measured against any yardstick, the psychological soundness and emotional appropriateness and helpfulness of the Jewish grief and mourning rituals are most impressive. Rabbi Spiro presents them fairly and objectively. He does not minimize what is unsound or even pathological that he finds in the Jewish culture pattern, but it is surprising how little of this there is. Rabbi Spiro does not undertake a comparison of the mourning rituals and customs of Judaism with those of other modern religions, although this might well make another fascinating volume. But we have only to recall the best-seller, *The American Way of Death*, to realize how pathological burial customs and practices can become when the secular and the commercial are given free rein. Rabbi Spiro makes a proper and timely plea for the restoration of strictly religious auspices in the conduct of Jewish burials, to avoid the environmental influences which are rampant around us.

We must all face at one time or other in our lives, the problem which arises on the death of a loved one. This constitutes a universal situation. We anticipate that parents and older siblings will pre-decease us. We expect that we shall be grievously assaulted and distressed by the unhappy event. We inevitably give many a thought to the subject in advance, no matter how loving and close our relations are.

In a sense, we begin our grieving long before the actuality, in the case of a particular person or persons, especially when a death is preceded by a long terminal illness, as it so often is. This is nature's way of preventing the sudden shock from overwhelming us completely.

However, the situation is exactly the opposite when the subject is our own demise. Psychoanalytic research, based upon individual and group experiences, reveals that no man can really contemplate his own death, or accept the fact that he shall ever cease to be. Saints seemingly contradict this by welcoming death, mystics by negating it, cynics by scoffing at it, and philosophers by rationalizing it. But the fact remains that the more deeply we delve into the psyche, the more this is confirmed.

One may say that the psychoanalytic dictum is seemingly contradicted by the fact that some people appear to spend all their days in fear of death. Suicide seems also to be a contradictory fact.

However, when we delve into the dynamics of the person who fears death, we find that usually what is involved is not really his own death, but that of another, against whom he unconsciously harbors a death-wish. But he feels he merits the ultimate punishment for having such wishes. This, and the guilt he would feel if his wish were to come true, accomplishes the turn-about which makes him fear his own death.

Psychologically, the threat or contemplation of suicide is most often really a disguised case of murder. The person feels outsized angers, resentments and even hatreds against a near one. However, the hated one is so greatly feared, loved or inaccessible by virtue of disease, distance or death, that he cannot put his aggressions on the right target, in the right amount, at the right time. They are then turned inward upon the self. Only by killing himself, can he kill the hated-loved one within himself, with whom he has completely identified. Thus, it is still not his own death, but that of another which he contemplates.

There are, nevertheless, a few instances where a person may actually contemplate his own death, but these are very rare. For example, when a person is incurably ill and suffering from unbearable pain, he may welcome death: but even in such cases, very few people ever actually commit suicide. Nature has a merciful mechanism, instead, which comes to their aid, allowing the curtain of oblivion to descend gradually and blot out consciousness. Likewise, a person who has suffered a shattering loss, whether of a dear one, a fortune of money, a position, or fame, may find life intolerable and may contemplate suicide. However, the impulse is relatively short-lived, and the person soon regains his will to live. Very few thwarted lovers ever jump off "Lover's Leap." They find another love, or make another fortune, or gain a new position, instead.

This leaves the few cases where a person "goes berserk" and turns the murder weapon against himself, after killing others. One would have to venture into the realm of psychiatric pathology to explain such behavior. It is not within the purview of the normal. We may, therefore, still agree that no one can really contemplate his own demise.

The death of a dear one, however, has to be faced and handled. There is no healthy way in which it can be ignored. The mourning customs which are prevalent in any culture are the means adopted by the individual and the community to handle this enormously disruptive and intolerable fact, and to enable the bereaved to absorb the shock and pain of it in manageable doses, and to go on living.

This is the major contribution which Rabbi Spiro has made, that he has broadened our knowledge and understanding of the Jewish way with death, has demonstrated how soundly rooted its principles are psychologically, and has sounded a call for the restitution of its pristine excellence. For this, his readers of all faiths will be grateful to him.

ABRAHAM N. FRANZBLAU

AAAPSS   The Annals of the American Academy of Po-
          litical and Social Science
BJMP   British Journal of Medical Psychology
CHL   Code of Hebrew Law (or, Shulchan Aruch,
          Yoreh Deah; the page numbers in the text
          refer to the English edition)
IJP   International Journal of Psycho-Analysis
JAOS   Journal of the American Oriental Society
JASP   Journal of Abnormal and Social Psychology
JE   Jewish Encyclopedia
KSA   Kitzur Shulchan Aruch
M   Mishnah
PQ   Psychoanalytic Quarterly
SA, YD   Shulchan Aruch, Yoreh Deah

Midrash Rabba:

Deut. R.   Deuteronomy Rabba
Eccl. R.   Ecclesiastes Rabba
Ex. R.   Exodus Rabba
Gen. R.   Genesis Rabba
Lam. R.   Lamentations Rabba
Lev. R.   Leviticus Rabba
Nu. R.   Numbers Rabba

Talmud:

AZ   Avodah Zara
BB   Baba Batra
Ber.   Berachot
BK   Baba Kama
BM   Baba Metzia

Erub.	Erubin
Ket.	Ketubot
Mak.	Makkot
Meg.	Megillah
Mid.	Middot
MK	Moed Katan
Ned.	Nedarim
San.	Sanhedrin
Sem.	Semachot
Shabb.	Shabbat
Yeb.	Yebamot
Zeb.	Zebachim

Introduction

Grief is the expression of sorrow or the emotional response to a bereavement while *mourning* is the means
whereby the bereaved person attempts to handle the suffering and emotional distress caused by bereavement.
Through psychological insight we can gain a deeper comprehension of the functioning of grief within the individual. Mourning applies more to cultural aspects of grief
while the group or society in which the individual lives
provides the techniques for handling grief. Mourning involves the techniques utilized; that is, the way the bereaved person handles his grief.

Grief requires understanding within a psychological
framework. It is important, also, to apply this understanding to the Jewish sources to see if Judaism accounts for the
psychological meaning of grief and to identify and define
the Jewish concepts in regard to grief.

The psychological concepts are not explicit in the Jewish

sources. We can only define them through an attempt to elucidate the human motivation which prompted the laws, illustrations, and aphorisms that we find and interpret their psychological meaning. This may give us the key to the understanding of Jewish legislation and ritual concerning bereavement while still allowing for the possible validity of non-psychological interpretations.

As we seek the meaning of grief within a psychological framework and apply our observations to the Jewish sources, five dominant themes will emerge in the following pages:

1. The primary sources of the grief reaction are unconscious and grow out of the inherent dynamic structure of the individual. The two opposing forces of love and aggressiveness continually contend with each other. In the grief situation this polarity causes two basic reactions: frustration because the force of love is suddenly thwarted by the death of the loved one, and guilt resulting from aggressive impulses.

2. The conflict between frustration and guilt gives rise in turn to a state of anxiety. The bereaved, overwhelmed by the distress of this conflict, seeks in self-preservaton to protect himself from emotional collapse and resorts to the employment of various defenses which may help his cause. The bereaved first uses the defense of denial. He rejects reality by refusing to believe that the loved object has really died. Using the defense of repression, the bereaved endeavors to reduce the painful feelings of conflict by pushing out of consciousness all thoughts associated with the death of the loved object. The bereaved may also use the defense of regression to an earlier stage of life when a

certain mechanism of confronting a loss may have been successful. Two other defenses frequently employed, which hinder rather than help the mourner in his attempt to recover from the loss and readjust to life, are self-punishment and projection. They only disguise the feelings of the mourner and direct them into potentially harmful channels.

3. Judaism as a sociocultural system, in providing specific laws, rites, and mores of mourning, and establishing definite time sequences, does not deny the need for the various defenses, but prevents them from becoming pathological. Death is accepted as a reality; hence the defense of denial cannot be employed for long. Repressed feelings are rechannelled through the active observance of the various ceremonials. The defense of regression, usually revealed in a feeling of helplessness, which carries over into helpless behavior on the part of the mourner, is at first allowed full expression in the Jewish provisions for mourning. But gradually the mourner assumes more responsibility with regard to the details of his daily life, and the regressive behavior disappears. The defense of self-punishment (which in other cultures sometimes takes the form of physical mutilation or even suicide) is channelled instead in Judaism into abstention and other types of self-denial which assuage the mourner's guilt for his aggressive impulses and prevent him from hurting himself or projecting his hostility. Thus the mourner is helped to use his defenses in the service of his grief-work.

4. Judaism, as a sociocultural system, tries to resolve the conflicts of grief by rechannelling love impulses and alleviating feelings of guilt, in the following ways:

a. The mourner may not disguise the fact that the loved object is really dead, but must realistically face the inescapability of death.

b. Through the observances and ceremonies which the mourner carries out, he is enabled to lean upon his sociocultural system, confident that it has cultural authority and divine sanction. Thus he feels he is doing the right thing and he knows exactly what is expected of him. This reduces confusion, which can only hinder the mourning process.

c. The mourner has not only the freedom but the right to express his deepest feelings of grief. This minimizes the possibility of denying the death or ignoring the reality of the loss or the emotional conflicts which it engenders. Moreover, by expressing his grief, he gradually learns to detach himself from the deceased and develop new relationships and interests.

5. Most of the laws and rituals of Judaism—as well as its values and beliefs—are developed around a communal or social structure. Since the key to the therapeutic efficacy of mourning is the ability of the mourner to transfer his dependency needs and love impulses to other persons and objects, the Jewish sociocultural system gives him abundant opportunity to accomplish this. The mourner does not perform the mourning rites in isolation, but as an active member of the group. This gives the mourner the opportunity to detach himself from the deceased and to experience a sense of acceptance by his community. This helps him to transfer his ties of love and to alleviate his feelings of guilt. The community conveys to him a feeling of being genuinely needed, which is therapeutic since the mourner

often feels neglected and unwanted after the death of his loved one. Judaism thus handles the problems of bereavement through the social experience, enabling the mourner to accept the challenge of life without his loved one and reconstruct a wholesome pattern of living for himself.

There is, in Judaism, a time to die, a time to lose, a time to break down, a time to weep, a time to rend, and a time to mourn—but also a time to heal and a time to gather stones together.

Acknowledgments

I wish to express my gratitude to Professors Alexander Guttman and Robert L. Katz who offered many helpful suggestions and corrections in the original manuscript; to Dr. Norman J. Levy and Dr. Abraham N. Franzblau for their valuable observations.

I am indebted to my wife Marilyn whose companionship is a constant source of inspiration. I am also thankful to the members of Temple Anshe Emeth for their support and encouragement.

My appreciation is extended to the following authors and publishers for permission to quote from their works: Carroll A. Wise, *Pastoral Counseling*, (Harper & Row); Paul E. Irion, *The Funeral and the Mourners*, and Edgar N. Jackson, *Understanding Grief*, (Abingdon Press); Gert Heilbrunn, article "On Weeping," in *The Psychoanalytic Quarterly*; Herman Feifel (editor), *The Meaning of Death*, (McGraw-Hill Book Company); Karl Abraham,

Selected Papers on Psychoanalysis (Basic Books, Inc.); Sigmund Freud, "Mourning and Melancholia" in *Collected Papers*, Volume IV, and *New Introductory Lectures* (The Hogarth Press); Hayyim Schauss, *The Lifetime of a Jew*, and Jacob D. Schwarz (editor), *Responsa of the Central Conference of American Rabbis* (Union of American Hebrew Congregations); Rollo May, *Man's Search for Himself*, and Otto Fenichel, *The Psychoanalytic Theory of Neurosis* (W. W. Norton & Company, Inc.); Erich Lindemann, "Symptomatology and Management of Acute Grief," *The American Journal of Psychiatry; The Soncino Talmud; The Midrash Rabbah* (The Soncino Press, London, England).

I also wish to thank the Hebrew Union College-Jewish Institute of Religion for permitting me to adapt the manuscript originally submitted as a doctoral dissertation.

PART ONE

The Psychological Meaning of Bereavement

I

The Sources of Grief

Introduction. When death occurs, the emotional consti-
tution of the bereaved person undergoes drastic alterations
related to deep psychic patterns developed in the past and
techniques used previously for confronting deprivation and
separation. Many emotional forces come to the surface and
are manifested in the grief responses. We must begin by in-
vestigating these forces which interact to produce the
effects of bereavement.

The emotional capital invested in the loss of a loved object can be great. The forces which produce the emotional
effects of bereavement must also be profound. Is it sufficient to say that the mourner grieves simply because he
misses the loved person and is lonely, or is there more to
bereavement behavior than this?

Some basic psychoanalytic theories directly relate to the
question.

The Dynamic Personality. One of the essential ways in

which psychoanalysis is distinguished from descriptive psychology is its concept of "forces" or "drives" operating within the psyche. The two most basic are the sex drive and the aggressive drive, both of which are present from birth. The infant possesses sexual forces which pass through three basic stages in its early development. First is the "oral stage," in which the principal desires of the infant center on the mouth as the erogenous zone of excitation. Second is the "anal stage," during which the infant receives erotic pleasure from sphincter movements—both the retention and expulsion of the feces. In the third or "phallic stage," the child's interests focus mainly on the genital zone.

The erotic impulse is present throughout all three stages but receives a different emphasis in each. When a new phase begins, the characteristics of the previous phase do not necessarily end, but the amount of psychic energy spent on it merely diminishes. By the time the phallic stage is completed and the next period of growth, the "latency period," begins, there is incorporated within the psychic structure residuals of all three stages: the oral, the anal, and the phallic.

The psychic or emotional energy associated with the sex drive is known as "libido" or "libidinal energy." In each of the three stages, the libido is focused in a different psychological area. The term "libidinal energy" does not refer only to the urge towards sexual union. Freud meant to convey much more, as he states:

The nucleus of what we mean by love naturally consists (and this is what is commonly called love, and

*what the poets sing of) in sexual love with sexual
union as its aim. But we do not separate from this—
what in any case has a share in the name "love"—on
the one hand, self-love, and on the other, love for
parents and children, friendship, and love for human-
ity in general, and also devotion to concrete objects
and to abstract ideas.*[1]

The concept of libido emphasizes the "dynamic" characteristic of psychoanalytic theory. Through libido the psychic
energy is in continual flux. It may be directed, in the early
years, towards one of the three erogenous zones; it may be
directed towards oneself ("narcissism") or towards another person or thing ("object-love").

The other major drive or instinct is the aggressive drive,
in which two basic tendencies operate. One is the masochis-
tic impulse; that is, the urge to destroy or injure onself.
The second is its counterpart, the sadistic impulse; that is,
directed outwards towards other objects or things.

One of the original hypotheses of dynamic psychology is
that the mental structure may be compared to an iceberg,
only one-sixth of which is visible while five-sixths remains
under the surface. Dynamic psychology emphasizes that
most of our mental functioning is below the level of conscious awareness. The dynamic "Unconscious" determines
in large measure our seemingly conscious thoughts and actions. In the grief response, psychoanalysis maintains, most
of the mourner's reactions to a bereavement are dependent
on the forces of the Unconscious. The Unconscious also
comprises the memories, impressions, and phantasies that
grow out of the whole experience of life.

Another formulation of the psychic processes helps to make the vital connection between unconscious forces and behavior patterns more understandable. This is the "structural hypothesis," which consists of three major divisions: the id, ego, superego. These divisions may be helpful in understanding the grief process.

The "id" is that aspect of the psyche which contains the source of instinctive energy and libido, and is an energy system itself. The sex and aggressive instincts struggle with each other there. It is completely unaware, chaotic, non-logical, non-rational, acting with no purpose save one: the gratification of its libidinal and aggressive urges. The id strives at all times to attain as much pleasure as possible and to avoid or draw away from any event or process which may involve unpleasant effects, such as bereavement.

The "superego" functions as a kind of conscience, built up principally from early childhood experiences through incorporation of parental prohibitions and commands. It contains some of the energy of the id and acts with similar impulses. However, once it is formed the impulses of the superego oppose those of the id. While the id strives for direct and complete gratification of its desires, the superego strives to control these desires. As an example of this phenomenon, the id may urge the individual to destroy or hate another person while the superego may react by demanding that the person be admired or loved instead.

The "ego" consists of the organized processes of the mind. Here is the seat of our perceptions and our consciousness or awareness of the external world. Here is the source of rationality and the perception of reality. The ego holds an uneasy position between the id and superego, endeavoring to mediate the demands of both. Because the ego deals with adjustment to the external world, it must usually struggle with the drives and impulses which comprise the inner world of id and superego. The ego is essentially the "I" of self of which each person is aware as he functions in life. In the grief response, the conflict between the ego and id on the one hand, and the ego and superego, on the other, reaches a high point.

The Loss of Love. It was originally thought that the id accounted for the entire psychic apparatus at birth. It is now thought that both the id and the ego are derived from a "primordial substrate." The eventual separation of the two is caused by modifications imposed on the id from the individual's environment, but they are never completely separated. One of the prime functions of the ego is to bring the outside world to the aid of the id for the gratification of instinctual needs. The pressure of the environment alone differentiates the ego from the id. But since the id works only for its own gratification, the burden of developing harmony and equilibrium falls upon the ego. To use Freud's analogy, the ego in its relation to the id is "like a man on horseback who has to hold in check the superior strength of the horse . . ." [2] And since the horse is sometimes wild, the ego finds itself in conflict and tension with the id.

The ego-id conflict begins during early infancy. The very young infant lacks discernment between external and internal stimuli. In the early months of life, the individual is narcissistic; that is, all stimuli are experienced as emanating from the infant itself, and all libidinal energy is directed to self-gratification. The sources of gratification which the infant continually desires—such as the bottle or breast or the warm embrace of the mother—are all experienced as being an inseparable part of the infant.

The distinction between the outer and inner worlds does not begin until the infant experiences repeated frustration. There are times when it desires to be fed, but food is not offered. It desires warmth, but the mother is not present to satisfy its needs. Moreover, there may be noxious stimuli acting upon the infant, such as cold or dampness. Through experiencing lack of gratification or uncomfortable stimuli, it eventually realizes that there are stimuli which come from outside of itself. Frustration thus causes the distinction to be made between the external world and the internal world, and thus the individual's ability to perceive reality develops. The ego can then act effectively in the interests of the id, and can utilize the environment for id gratification.

However, this sense of reality (or "reality principle") dictates that the impulse of the id must at times be frustrated. Because of external necessity, the ego may have to postpone immediate gratification. But the id cares nothing about external necessity or future pleasure. The id knows only the demands of immediacy. This leads to conflict between the ego and the id.

When such a conflict arises, the ego attempts to control the id rather than to operate in its service. There are times when it feels compelled to master the raw forces that seek immediate satisfaction rather than to function only as their "executant." The ego is capable of becoming master of the id since it draws its own energic force from the same reservoir of psychic energy. In spite of this, the id continues its relentless struggle for immediate discharge, which sets up a continual tension within the ego.

Because of this struggle of the id to discharge its energy, it sometimes happens that the ego temporarily becomes the servant rather than the master or executant of the id. The forces within the id then win out, in spite of the ego's attempt to conquer or control. This condition occurs in traumatic situations when the ego is overwhelmed by the feeling of helplessness. As Freud has stated: ". . . the protective barrier against external stimuli has been broken through and over-great quantities of excitation impinge upon the mental apparatus . . ." [3] A trauma is a danger situation which makes such a tremendous impact on the psyche that the energy held within the id is discharged with immediacy and acceleration. The most significant of these danger situations is, according to dynamic psychology, the "loss of the loved object." [4]

In bereavement, the libidinal energy of the id which was directed towards the loved object is suddenly interrupted by death. It continues to seek satisfaction although the object of its satisfaction no longer exists. It is as if the ego were caught behind a broken dam with the forceful water rushing at it. The death of a loved object destroys the equilibrium between the ego and the id, and the ego then finds it difficult and painful, if not impossible, to cope with the libidinal energy that seeks discharge.

When the ego is overwhelmed in this way it feels helpless. It is at this point, after the death of a loved object, when the ego fears it may be overwhelmed with the threat of collapse, that anxiety arises. But in accord with the principle of self-preservation it cannot allow itself merely to collapse or be destroyed by the libidinal force of the id. On the contrary, it must do something about this force.

Ambivalence. The first source of the grief-response involves the sex or love instinct, the second arises out of the aggressive instinct. That aggression is a natural impulse within the psyche can be seen in dreams which reveal death wishes. Freud has pointed out that such dreams often mean that the dreamer has wished the close relative dead at some time in the past, especially during childhood.[5] Although consciously the dreamer would be grieved by the death, the dream expresses the hostile impulses that are felt along with love impulses. There is a natural interplay within the psyche between the sex instinct and the aggressive instinct. It is human to feel ambivalence towards the same object, to possess "conflicting feelings of tenderness and hostility." [6]

These natural feelings of ambivalence are a common phenomenon in the dreams of bereaved persons. According to Anderson, these dreams can be divided into two types.[7] In one, the dead person may be attempting to destroy the dreamer, or the dreamer may be performing destructive acts against the dead. In the second type, the deceased is alive and past experiences of a happy nature are re-enacted. In other words, the bereaved person feels both hostility, which is revealed in the destructive activity in the dream, and also love, which expresses itself through the restoration of life to the deceased. It is obvious that the ambivalence is derived from interplay of the two basic instincts.

Ambivalence is, therefore, at the very heart of the emotional response to the loss of a loved object. These conflicting feelings are bound to be present after a death, since they were present during the entire relationship between the bereaved and the deceased. In the case of a spouse, where the relationship came into existence only after the formative years of psychic development had passed, is ambivalence especially strong? The answer is that ambivalence towards a spouse is not as strong as towards a parent because the relationship does not emanate from early childhood.

The development of ambivalence does not begin until the latter part of the oral stage. While the aggressive instinct may be operating at birth, there are no feelings of ambivalence then. The early part of the oral stage is really an autoerotic sucking stage, and the infant possesses no awareness of external objects. Without external objects there can be no ambivalence. Ambivalence is not felt until the latter part of the oral stage when the infant desires to incorporate everything desirable, even to the point of destroying it. The infant does not do this because of sadistic impulses but because it is the way to receive oral gratification. The destruction of something desirable is, therefore, of an "objective" nature.

Incorporation can be the means of decreasing the distance between infant and object. The natural expression of repulsion and hatred is to spit out the undesirable object. This is really the first instance of negative behavior since incorporation is natural and objective, and only secondarily destructive.[8] As a primary process, incorporation is a way of holding to the desired object; by taking it in, it is not lost. Since the first profound pain that the infant feels is that of separation from the mother during weaning, it is this oral separation that has to be relieved. The natural method of relief is re-incorporation; the infant needs to take in, to relieve the pain experienced.

The process of incorporation (or its complement, expulsion) is related to the child's total perception of reality.[9] The first experience to disturb the child's equilibrium and peaceful sleep is hunger. This forces him to become aware of the outside world since it is outside of himself that he must seek satisfaction. Thus he initially relates to reality through incorporation of food to satisfy his hunger. The child's experience with taking in food or expelling it becomes the prototype for all later perceptions of reality. When a person suffers a bereavement, he may tend to return to this very early stage and to the techniques adopted for the handling of hunger.

The grown person seeks to identify with the deceased, utilizing incorporation and thereby internalizing the loved object. In early infancy, too, all desirable objects are identified with the self. They should be a part of the self since they are desirable. In infancy all libidinal energy is directed to other objects as well. But when bereavement occurs, the energy which is directed to the loved object turns inward to the self, once again. This accounts for the internalization of the deceased within the bereaved person, and the identification of the bereaved with the deceased, the latter becoming a part of him. As Fenichel has stated, "by incorporating objects one becomes united with them." [10] The process further accounts for such expressions as "I love you so much I could eat you up" or "In your death something in me also dies."

The process of identification can have unwholesome manifestations. The personality of the bereaved person may become more identified with the deceased than with himself. This can occur when the intensity of grief is so great that the thought of having lost the loved object cannot be tolerated.[11] Erich Lindemann regards it as a pathological reaction for a bereaved person to develop personality traits too similar to those of the deceased. This impulse to identify can go so far that the bereaved takes on the symptoms of the deceased during the final illness.[12]

Incorporation or introjection is primarily a means of holding on to and preserving the loved object; it is only secondarily destructive. The destructive aspect is not predominant in the oral stage. With the advent of the anal stage, ambivalence reaches greater development with the prevalence of the destructive aspect. The elimination of feces is destructive, the child receiving pleasure from the "pinching off" of feces and thereby satisfying a sadistic impulse.[13] But the child also receives pleasure from holding on to the feces, and not eliminating it. He therefore finds satisfaction in both retention and expulsion. From this anal experience, the child learns to relate to loved objects in a contradictory manner—the feces represents, in a sense, a loved object, and also an object to be relinquished.

During the anal period, the contradictory feelings towards the feces lead to ambivalent feelings towards the mother. It is the mother who guides the child in sphincter control and training. At times the child's wishes conflict with the mother's; she may try to persuade the child to eliminate the feces when the child does not wish to. Conflictual feelings of love and hate towards his mother are thus imbued in the child.

Abraham points out that in many mourners there are anal symptoms when the death of a loved object occurs. He states that "news of the death of a near relative will often set up in a person a violent pressure in his bowels as if the whole of his intestines were being expelled, or as if something was being torn away inside him and was going to come out through his anus." He further maintains that this symptom is an archaic reaction and expresses itself along with the expression of grief.[14]

The condition of ambivalence towards loved objects is deeply rooted in the psyche. According to Winnicott, it is "a clash which is inevitable if loving is to include the instinctual element that belongs to it."[15] Each person varies in his ability to regulate the conflicts universally characteristic of the psyche.

The Burden of Guilt. One of the basic methods employed by the psyche for the purpose of subduing ambivalence is the counteraggressiveness of the superego. The superego is the internalized authority of parents and parent surrogates. It is largely unconscious and relentlessly demanding. Like the id, it does not operate rationally but drives for the satisfaction of its demands.

When the child feels hostility towards a parent or other loved object, the object of authority may scold or denounce him for his negative feelings. The child grows to dread his aggressive feelings, which, to him, threaten the loss of love. He must control his aggressiveness if he wants to maintain the love and approval of this object. To quote Freud, there develops "the erection of an internal authority, and instinctual renunciation due to dread of it—that is, dread of conscience."[16] This dread of conscience is the same as the sense of guilt.

The superego is the seat of morality or conscience, and

the ego may feel threatened by the morality-demands made by the superego. This becomes all the more intense if the aggressiveness felt towards loved objects is great. It may be said that the more ambivalence felt and internalized the more rigid and authoritarian the conscience (or superego).

Regardless of the degree of rigidity, every person inevitably experiences some sense of guilt as a consequence of the development of the superego. Since the superego does not function with awareness or rationality, it does not differentiate between an intention and a deed. In other words, when the child wishes that his father were dead or that he could hurt his sibling, to the superego this wish is the same as its fulfillment. As Freud has stated,

> . . . *the omniscience of the super-ego robbed the distinction between intended aggressions and aggressions committed of its significance; a mere intention to commit an act of violence could then evoke a sense of guilt . . .*[17]

The lack of distinction between wish and deed, which breeds guilt, is seen in the case presented by Winnicott of a girl who suffered a deep depression subsequent to her father's death.[18] The father had purchased a car during a period in the girl's life when she was experiencing feelings of intense hostility towards him, mixed with feelings of love. He took her for a ride in the car, and an accident occurred in which the father was killed. This brought on the depression. It was inferred from this situation that the girl's wish to kill her father and his actual death were equated unconsciously in her mind; she therefore condemned herself as responsible for his death. Her superego had made no distinction, and she consequently suffered the guilt imposed upon her by her conscience.

The ego appears to suffer particularly from feelings of guilt which result from the death wish, because then the superego becomes all the more relentless in its demanding and persecutory role, in view of its equation of intention with action. There are times in the life of every person when he has had aggressive and/or death wishes against a loved object. These wishes usually remain unconscious and are experienced through the sense of guilt. However, when the loved object dies the ego feels, through the influence of the superego, that the person's death wishes were realized. Thus, the bereaved person actually feels he has caused the death, either directly or indirectly. Moreover, the hostile feelings, repressed or ignored while the deceased still lived, emerge and become conscious at the time of death, along with the release of other emotional forces during the expression of grief. This intensifies the sense of guilt and causes it to be all the more painful to the bereaved.[19]

The intensification of guilt may also be caused by the thwarting of undischarged libidinal energy. The death of a loved object interferes with the id's drive to receive libidinal satisfaction, which may in turn produce greater hostility towards the deceased. The id, in this case, having no awareness or rationality, holds the dead person responsible for the frustration. But this new development of aggressiveness towards the now-dead loved object must be controlled, and the superego heightens the sense of guilt.[20]

Guilt imposed by the superego can express itself in

several ways. The guilt-ridden person may feel that he is personally responsible for the death of the loved object. Or he may feel that his hostile impulses towards the loved object made the latter's life more difficult. He may also look upon the death as a punishment because of his past aggressiveness, arising out of the frustration of libidinal energy directed towards the deceased. The occurrence of death intensifies guilt since it is then too late to rectify ambivalent feelings and hostility impulses.

This intensification of guilt can lead to a state of anxiety similar to that felt as a result of frustrated libidinal forces. We will discuss this form of anxiety in the next chapter.

Conclusion. We have noted that psychoanalytic theory postulates two basic instincts or drives within the individual: the sex drive and the aggressive drive. The first (*eros*) leads the individual to unite as closely as possible with his loved object while the second (*thanatos*) causes the individual to hate and wish to destroy.

The libidinal energy that demands satisfaction is derived from the sex instinct. This energy is located within the unconscious id. When the ego feels unable to cope with the demands of the id for gratification, the ego is threatened. This threat to the ego creates a state of anxiety.

The individual is also possessed of aggressive feelings towards the loved object, derived from the aggressive instinct. When this aggressiveness was displayed as a child, the individual was punished. This punishment by outside authorities became internalized eventually as the superego or conscience and is expressed by feelings of guilt. When the death of a loved object occurs, the sense of guilt is intensified. As the superego heightens its punishing influence, the ego is threatened once more. This threat to the ego by the superego creates a state of anxiety.

Thus, the painful experience of grief is derived from two basic sources within the psyche: the ego-id conflict and the ego-superego conflict. These two conflicts in turn emanate from the two opposing instincts: the sex instinct and the aggressive instinct. Both conflicts come to a head, subsequent to the loss of a loved object, in the state of anxiety.

1. Quoted in W. Healy, A. F. Bronner, and A. M. Bowers, *The Structure and Meaning of Psychoanalysis* ("Judge Baker Foundation," No. 6; New York: Alfred E. Knopf, Co., 1930), p. 4.

2. Sigmund Freud, "The Ego and the Id" (*A General Selection from the Works of Sigmund Freud*, ed. John Rickman, Garden City, New York: Doubleday Anchor Books, 1957), p. 215.

3. Freud, *Inhibition, Symptoms and Anxiety*, trans. Alix Strachey (London: The Hogarth Press Ltd., 1948), p. 94.

4. *Ibid.*, p. 106.

5. Sigmund Freud, *The Interpretation of Dreams*, trans., A. A. Brill (New York: The Modern Library, 1950), pp. 148–149.

6. Freud, "Totem and Taboo" (*The Basic Writings of Sigmund Freud*, trans. & ed. A. A. Brill, New York: The Modern Library, 1938), p. 818; also, Freud, *Civilization and its Discontents*, trans. Joan Riviere (London: The Hogarth Press, 1939), pp. 102–103.

7. Charles Anderson, "Aspects of Pathological Grief and Mourning," *IJP*, XXX (1949), pp. 49–53.

8. Otto Fenichel, *The Psychoanalytic Theory of Neurosis* (New York: W. W. Norton & Company, Inc., 1945), pp. 38 and 83; see also p. 64 and Karl Abraham, *Selected Papers on Psychoanalysis*, trans. Douglas Bryan and Alix Strachey (New York: Basic Books, Inc., Publishers, 1957), p. 473.

9. Edward Glover, "The Significance of the Mouth in Psychoanalysis," *BJMP*, IV (1924), p. 141; Fenichel, *op. cit.*, p. 63.

10. Fenichel, *op. cit.*, p. 63; see also Freud, *Group Psychology and the Analysis of the Ego*, trans., James Strachey (New York: Bantam Books, Inc., 1960), pp. 49–50.

11. Edgar N. Jackson, *Understanding Grief* (New York and Nashville: Abingdon Press, 1957), p. 63.

12. Erich Lindemann, "Symptomatology and Management of Acute Grief," *AJP*, CI, No. 2 (September, 1944), pp. 142–143.

13. Fenichel, *op. cit.*, p. 66; see Jeno Harnik, "Introjection and Projection in the Mechanism of Depression," *IJP*, XIII (1932), p. 95; also Healy *et al.*, op. cit., p. 95.

14. Abraham, *op. cit.*, pp. 426–427.

15. Donald W. Winnicott, "Psyche-Analysis and the Sense of Guilt," *Psycho-Analysis and Contemporary Thought*, ed. J. D. Sutherland ("The International Psycho-Analytical Library," No. 53. London: The Hogarth Press, 1958), p. 18.

16. Freud, *Civilization and its Discontents*, pp. 113–115; *Totem and* Taboo, pp. 860; Fenichel, *op. cit.*, p. 134.

17. *Civilization and its Discontents*, p. 129; *Totem and Taboo*, pp. 859–867; also Fenichel, *op. cit.*, p. 359.

18. Winnicott, *op. cit.*, p. 18.

19. Freud, *Group Psychology and the Analysis of the Ego*, p. 52; William F. Rogers, *Ye shall be Comforted* (Philadelphia: Westminster Press, 1950), p. 20.

20. *Civilization and its Discontents*, pp. 130–131; John Bowlby applies this analysis to the child whose sense of guilt may lead to a desire for greater love which, if not met, leads to more frustration and intensified guilt ("Psycho-Analysis and Child Care," *Psycho-Analysis and Contemporary Thought*, p. 38).

II

The Dynamics of Grief

Introduction. We have seen in the previous chapter that the emotional suffering experienced by the mourner is basically a result of two forces deeply conflicting with the ego.

Anxiety itself is not the end result of the disturbing forces. Anxiety in turn produces emotional consequences in the form of "ego defenses." It communicates to the ego that there is trouble, and the ego must defend itself employing a variety of defenses for its safety and its preservation. The bereaved person, as a result of the threatening forces which arise due to the death of a loved object, uses these common defenses.

The Meaning of Anxiety. Anxiety is a feeling of intense dread, a feeling that the total self is threatened. This painful state is also a reaction of helplessness to a traumatic situation. In the case of bereavement, the loss of the loved object is the traumatic situation.

In bereavement the libidinal force has lost its aim in the person of the loved object; as a consequence this force turns overwhelmingly towards the ego. There is no other direction for it to take. In addition, the ego must also contend with the punitive force of the superego which manifests itself in the form of painful feelings of guilt.

Fenichel explains how these two conflictual forces produce a traumatic situation:

> *The basic function of the mental apparatus is the re-establishment of stability after a disturbance of external stimuli . . . Whenever the maintenance of a (relative) equilibrium fails, a state of emergency arises. Too high an influx of excitement within the given unit of time is the simplest type of such an emergency.*[1]

In the condition of bereavement, the high influx of excitement emanates from both the id and the superego, disturbing the stability of the ego.

Because of the emergency and immediacy of the situation, the ego is not prepared to accept the conflicts which ensue. Fenichel further states, ". . . an incident is likely to have a traumatic effect in direct relationship to the unexpectedness with which it occurs . . ."[2] An individual is rarely completely ready for the death of a loved object. The unexpectedness, and therefore the shock to the ego, is that much more overwhelming.

When the sudden emergency of death occurs, the ego awkwardly attempts to re-establish a balance. But the forces against it are so powerful that the great strain only causes more painful sensations of tension and apprehension.

The ego must utilize all its energies to control the forces of the id and superego.

The bereaved individual feels as though his very existence is threatened. The utilization and intensification of all the energies of the ego only creates a weakening effect, which is a further threat to the bereaved person. There seems to be no way out for the ego; it feels trapped by the powerful stimuli suddenly thrust upon it. The consequence of this traumatic situation is the state of anxiety.

In the state of anxiety, the individual experiences a feeling of helplessness and a sense of intense apprehension and dread. This is bewildering to the bereaved peson because it is not the actual death itself which has created the state of anxiety, but rather the inability of the ego to control and master the conflictual threats which develop as a result of the death. Being unaware of the unconscious forces which arise from the depths of the id and superego, the painful feelings of anxiety disturb him. Fear knows its cause, but anxiety does not.

The individual who suffers from anxiety experiences the feeling of emptiness and weakness. It frequently happens that the anxiety-ridden individual goes through a state of passivity because of the extreme enervation experienced by the ego. There may be respiratory difficulties in addition to cardiac, vasomotor, and alimentary disturbances. There is often an increased pulse rate with accompanying feelings of insecurity and restlessness. Moreover, anxiety often causes the need to cry. These physical and emotional symptoms are comparable to the grief-responses. The intense suffering of grief is a result of a traumatic situation, just as anxiety is.

Freud points out that "every stage of development has its own particular conditions for anxiety; that is to say, a danger-situation appropriate to it." [3] He considers that to be the experience of birth, known as the "birth trauma," the prototype for all future conditions of anxiety. A basic threat to the child is separation from his mother, first experienced when the infant is separated from the warmth and security of its intrauterine existence. That experience stamps in the characteristic responses to trauma in the form of anxiety, which accompany the individual throughout life. The loss and severance which the infant experiences on leaving his existence in the womb, the bereaved person experiences with the death of a loved object. Both birth and death are traumatic situations which create anxiety.

Anxiety, however, must not be thought of as completely unwholesome and detrimental. It serves an important function in warning the ego of the threat to its existence. Sometimes the anxiety is the result of a neurotic condition and, hence, it is irrational. But in the case of death involving a loved object it serves a useful purpose to the ego, that of self-preservation. It arises to protect the ego from the threatening forces and stimuli resulting from the death of a loved object. The severe pain in itself makes the anxiety effective, since it compels the ego to protect itself, employing whatever method will allay the tension and apprehension the most. What the ego really must subdue are the threatening id and superego conflicts. Since these forces are unconscious, the method employed by the ego (the "defenses" or the "defense mechanisms") is also unconscious.

Denial, Repression and Regression. The first of these defenses is "denial." On learning of the death of a loved object, a common reaction is to deny the reality of the death saying "I don't believe it" or "it isn't true." The ego says "No" to a real situation which is imminently overwhelming. This defense is usually short-lived.

The most common and effective of all defenses is that of "repression." The ego makes the attempt to exclude completely from consciousness the painful impulses that struggle for release. The impulses do not disappear, however, but continue to seek satisfaction and release in the Unconscious. The ego engages in the struggle to hold these impulses in check, thereby consuming its own energy. It is also concerned with repressing the affective or feeling state which these impulses cause. The defense of repression is an ongoing process throughout life. Whenever some experience, feeling, thought or relationship is undesirable or threatens to disrupt the equilibrium of the psyche, the defense of repression is employed to keep from consciousness what is unwanted.

Repression is an important factor in the mental and emotional state of the bereaved person. When the loss of a loved object occurs, a multitude of undesirable and painful impulses rush toward discharge. The bereaved may have experienced negative feelings towards the deceased, feelings of hostility, jealousy, and perhaps death-wishes, which were repressed. But when the trauma of bereavement occurs, they struggle for release and recognition. It is here that repression plays its role for the ego by keeping the negative impulses unconscious.

Repression is also used by the bereaved to banish that which is painfully conscious. When death occurs, the great libidinal energy directed towards the loved object is suddenly frustrated, and the bereaved person tries to thrust out of consciousness the painful effect of the loss. Repression is especially strong in those cultures which do not provide the bereaved with a mode of dealing with the loss. Even in cultures which do provide effective mourning symbols and rituals, bereavement may strike a person with such immediacy that it is difficult to avoid repression completely.

Repression is not an emotionally satisfying solution to the loss of the loved object. The impulses are not discharged by it but are only held back, and the drives seek expression through other channels.

Another defense, common in the bereavement situation, is "regression." This is one of the prime reasons for the mourner's feeling of dependence, for the attention that he needs, and for the difficulty many mourners experience in relating maturely to other people.

The individual passes through several psychic stages in life, each with its own characteristics as we have mentioned.[4] One stage may be more "successful" than another; that is, the child may have less difficulty in his relationships to loved objects and to himself than in a preceding or succeeding stage. When a difficulty is encountered by the child, it is natural to return to a former stage when things were easier and less painful. This process is known as regression. The development of the child may be arrested at a difficult stage, a process known as "fixation."

A similar phenomenon may occur with the experience of bereavement. The painfulness of the undischarged forces and the sudden excitation may compel the ego to return to an earlier stage in its development, when it was able to handle the forces of the id. Thus, helplessness characteristic of bereavement may cause the bereaved person to regress to a period in his childhood when the methods available for handling conflicts seemed more successful. These methods may then be repeated by the bereaved person. It does not follow, however, that the childhood adjustive techniques will necessarily be successful now, when the bereaved person has passed that particular stage. It is this difficulty in the mechanism of regression that causes many of the problems which occur during the period of mourning, such as the inability to achieve a sense of independence or to relate to others with satisfaction.

Self-Punishment and Projection. Another defense resorted to by the bereaved, especially for the purpose of allaying feelings of guilt, is self-punishment or "turning against the self." [5] This is employed because the ego cannot tolerate the intense guilt felt as a result of the hostile impulses towards the deceased, which the ego displaces onto itself, in the form of punitive feelings and actions. Thus the energy of the aggressive forces is not lost but merely turned on the "aggressor." [6]

The employment of this defense can have serious consequences. One of the most significant reasons is that the turning within of aggression can really be a way for the ego to seek revenge against the loved object, by introjection of both the aggressive force and the loved object. As we have already noted,[7] the process of introjection can be a form of destruction. Thus, the bereaved person may be destroying the loved object because of the frustration and guilt that the latter caused through his death.[8]

While this process of "revenge" can occur, it is more

common for the "turning-against-the-self" defense to be employed by the ego as a means of achieving forgiveness from the deceased.[9] Since the superego causes the unpleasurable feelings of guilt, the ego seeks to appease the superego by showing remorse for the aggressive and ambivalent impulses. This feeling of sorrow is demonstrated to the superego in no more effective way than by abstention, reproach, punishment of a physical nature, and contrition. In other words, since the superego has injured the ego with the punitive effects of guilt, the ego attempts to appease the superego by employing forms of punishment against itself.

It is possible, of course, that a vicious circle may ensue from the employment of this defense. The superego punishes the ego with intensifying the sense of guilt. One of the reasons why mourning may be prolonged is the deep guilt felt and the difficulty of subduing it.

Another defense frequently employed by the bereaved is that of "projection," through which a person attributes to others his own unacceptable and undesirable wishes and impulses. The bereaved person may project his own hostile impulses onto the deceased in order to rid himself of them. This is an internal mental process carried out as though the feelings are thrust out onto the external world. The process takes place unconsciously, although the feeling arises in the conscious ego. However, the mechanism is remote and withdrawn from awareness and therefore seems to be separated from the ego and consciousness.[10]

The defense of projection may also be employed if the defense of "turning against the self" proves too painful in getting rid of the guilt imposed upon the mourner by his superego. Projection is then used to cast out not only the guilt but the punitive measures that may be directed against the self.[11]

If the process of projection is intensively employed by the bereaved person, then he will be convinced that the deceased really "possesses" hostile feelings and aggressive impulses against him. Like other defense mechanisms, projection may have serious consequences for emotional stability when employed unduly in the grief situation.

Through projection the mourner may come to consider the deceased as a cruel, avenging reality, giving justification for further hostility towards him. This increases hostility and more guilt follows, which in turn is projected again. Thus a vicious circle may ensue, and the bereaved may become convinced more than ever that the deceased is a "chastising and avenging fate." [12]

Consequently, the bereaved not only feels hatred towards the deceased but also fear and dread that the deceased will in some way harm the living. The ways are not necessarily brought to awareness. It may also happen that the aggressive forces directed against the deceased are themselves feared by the ego. But, through projection, this aggression will be feared in the form of the dead person.[13] Guilt and fear are therefore closely related through the process of projection. The greater the force of projection the greater the possibility for feelings of fear towards the deceased to develop, and the greater the intensity of guilt imposed upon the mourner by the superego.

Conclusion. The two primal forces of the psyche, love and aggression, conflict with the ego and produce the painful state of anxiety which actually warns the ego of the necessity of preserving itself from the threatening forces emanating from the id and superego. The most common method adopted by the ego to escape the overwhelming threat of anxiety is the employment of certain unconscious mechanisms of defense.

The five most common defenses employed by the ego as a result of bereavement are denial, repression, regression, self-punishment, and projection. The use of these defenses is not a real solution to the problems of the love-hate conflict, trauma, and anxiety. They are expedient ways adopted by the ego to prevent emotional collapse and to preserve itself in any way possible. Misused, however, each of the defenses can lead to further complications.

1. Fenichel, *op. cit.*, p. 117.

2. *Ibid.*, p. 118.

3. Freud, *New Introductory Lectures on Psycho-Analysis* ("The International Psycho-Analytical Library," No. 24; London: The Hogarth Press Ltd., 1957), p. 116.

4. *Supra*, pp. 7–8.

5. See J. C. Flugel, *Man, Morals and Society* (Harmondsworth, England: Penguin Books Ltd., 1955), p. 96.

6. Freud, "Mourning and Melancholia," *passim*.

7. *Supra*, p. 13.

8. Freud, *Group Psychology and the Analysis of the Ego*, p. 51.

9. Fenichel, *op. cit.*, p. 138.

10. G. Jelgersma, "Projection," *IJP*, VII (1926), 356.

11. Hermann Hunberg, "The Sense of Guilt and the Need for Punishment," *IJP*, VII (1926), 427.

12. Ibid., p. 431; Ernest Jones, "Fear, Guilt and Hate," *IJP*, X (1929), 384; Freud, *Totem and Taboo*, pp. 354–355.

13. Karin Stephen, "Introjection and Projection, Guilt and Rage," *BJMP*, XIV (1943), p. 329.

PART TWO

A Jewish Understanding of Grief

III

The Effects of
Bereavement

Introduction. Judaism is a cultural expression of the Jewish people. It is a set of laws, values, and beliefs, a mode of living developed and expressed by the Jewish people from Biblical times to the present. How does Judaism as a sociocultural system handle the emotional suffering engendered by the loss of a loved object? Does Judaism as a culture—through its laws, customs, rituals, and folkways —reflect insight into the deep suffering experienced by a bereaved individual? Do the therapeutic techniques it has developed over the course of time meet the needs of the mourner?

Does the Jewish tradition afford illustrations of the major characteristics of the grief-response previously investigated? Does Judaism provide for certain grief-responses which may be considered abnormal or distorted in the light of our previous discussion, revealing an inability of the mourner to

adjust to his new situation in life without the loved object?
These are the two basic questions of this chapter.

The Pain of Separation. According to the theory of the
libido, the intensity of the grief-response depends largely
on the degree of involvement between the bereaved and the
deceased prior to the death.[1] The amount of emotional
energy directed towards a person is based on the relationship with that person. When this relationship is suddenly
severed, the emotional energy is frustrated because its
object of satisfaction no longer exists. The permanent termination of an intense relationship produces the feelings of
grief.

First of all, Judaism does recognize the severe pain involved in the death of a loved object. In fact, grief is
thought of in terms of a fractured leg which needs slow
mending.[2] There is also the recognition that the painfulness
of grief is commensurate with the degree of interaction,
such as in the following: "There are degrees in mourning
depending upon the closeness of relationship." [3]

The fact that the complete severance of an intense relationship causes deep feelings of grief is brought out in the
Rabbinic dictum that if a mourner is observing "Shivah"
(the first seven days of mourning, beginning immediately
after the burial of the deceased) somewhere other than his
own home it is permissible for him to return to his home at
night in order to sleep.[4] The assumption of this law is that
the deceased, prior to his death, lived in the same home as
the bereaved, and that it was there that their relationship
became intensified. The home being a symbol of the relationship, this law shows that the Rabbis recognized that
sudden separation from the deceased is indeed painful. Returning to his own home at night, the total separation

would be more gradual, and the shock might not be so great. This is especially true during the night when the mourner is no longer in the presence of others who can comfort him. Although the trauma of losing a loved object cannot be avoided, it perhaps can be assuaged to some extent in this way.

The principle that the degree of grief is commensurate with the degree of involvement is seen again in the law that minors do not engage in mourning rites nor do they come into the category of "Chinuch" with regard to mourning.[5] This latter term refers to the training that minors received as they approached the age of majority in those religious matters that could not be observed until majority. Mourning, however, does not come into this category, probably because the Rabbis did not consider it sound for anyone to engage in limited mourning. The child is considered less capable of the deep feelings which overcome someone older as a result of losing a loved object. The libidinal attachments are not as strong, the ambivalent feelings not as intense. A child is more capable of transferring his libidinal attachments than the older person because these attachments are still variable. Since ambivalence has not developed in large measure, the feelings of guilt are therefore not as intense.

The age of thirteen for a boy or twelve years and one day [6] for a girl may be arbitrary ages for establishing the time when a person is required to mourn for a loved object. But these ages are usually the beginning of puberty when ambivalence and guilt become much stronger. From a "halachic" or legal point of view, however, these are the ages when the child becomes responsible for fulfilling all Jewish law, and mourning requirements are just one aspect of this responsibility. The leniency of the Halachah dealing with mourning is revealed in the regulation that even if a minor came of age during the period of Shivah, "the entire law of mourning lapses from him and he is not obligated therein." [7]

The intensity of interaction, which largely determines the degree of grief felt, also depends naturally on the amount of time spent with the loved object. Libidinal attachments grow stronger if the relationship extends over a long period of time. Because of this, the Halachah states that no mourning takes place for an infant less than thirty days old. There are three categories of infants up to one year of age, with respect to mourning obligations and rituals.

> *And they (the people) do not stand in line on the (immature) infant's account, nor do they (need) to recite the (usual) mourner's benediction, nor tender the (usual) condolence to the mourners. An infant thirty days old is taken forth (to burial) in a case. R. Judah says: Not a case that is borne on the shoulder, but one that is borne in the arms, and the people stand in line on its account, and recite the (additional) mourners' benediction and tender the (usual) condolence to the mourners. One twelve months old is taken forth (to burial) on a bier . . . R. Simeon b. Eleazar says, For any one that is taken out on a bier the public (should) show their distress.* [8]

The Rabbinic insight into the degree of emotional interaction also applies to betrothal. If one of the engaged pair dies, the pain of separation would not be as intense as if they were already married. The circumstances of betrothal have not allowed their relationship to become too intimate, and a minimal degree of grief would be felt. Hence, mourning is not required.[9]

The very opposite is true, however, in parent-child relationships. Even in Biblical times the prophets felt that the most grievous kind of mourning was that involving the death of an only son.[10] This is understandable when we recall that a male offspring was much more important to the father than a female not only in the Biblical period but throughout Jewish history. The son was taught by the father and was the guarantor for preserving the father's name. The relationship between father and son was always intimate and therefore the death of a son was that much more painful.

The converse of this relationship is also considered to be extremely intense. In the Talmud, the grief felt for a mother or father is considered the most painful kind.[11] In fact, the Rabbis disagreed with the prophets in their opinion as to which is the most grievous, the death of an offspring or the death of a parent. This difference is revealed in the laws of "keria." When a loved person died, a garment of the bereaved would be rent as a symbol of the pain involved in the separation. The Rabbis felt the loss of a parent to be greater by stating that if a father died the upper part of the garment is rent; if a son dies the lower part is torn. Eventually, the lower part (for the son) can be re-mended, but the upper part must remain rent (for the father).[12] The ritual itself recognizes that the grief felt for the father endures for a longer period and is more intense than that felt for a son.

The father is the personification of the superego, of the conscience. The father's commands and authority eventually become internalized in the developing child. It is the superego which causes the guilt felt in consequence of the death of a loved object, and it makes no distinction between thought and deed. If the child felt ambivalent towards the father while the latter was still living, this ambivalence may change to guilt feelings once the father is dead, and the punitive measures directed towards the ego by the superego are that much greater. Through its rituals Judaism accounts for the deeper pain of this separation compared with any other relationship.

In keeping with this, there are laws and rites especially directed to the bereaved offspring that do not affect any other mourner. The bereaved offspring may not wear pressed clothing until the first festival after the death or until he is rebuked because of his shabbiness. He may not cut his hair, engage in business or allow any feasting in his house until he is rebuked by others. In all other cases of mourners, these rituals remain in effect for a period of only thirty days at the most (known as "Shloshim" or "Thirty") after burial.[13]

This distinction is also seen once again in the laws of "keria." Ordinarily, after the death of a loved one the bereaved can either rend his garment by hand or with an instrument. But in the case of the death of a parent, the offspring must rend the garment with his hand. It is also optional ordinarily to divide the selvage-border of one's garment, but for an offspring it is a requirement. For anyone other than a deceased parent, the bereaved need only make a rent of a handbreadth, and it is only necessary to rend the uppermost garment that one is wearing. But for a parent, an offspring must tear the garment "till he bares his heart," and all the garments must be torn.[14] If the offspring rent his garment thinking that his parent had died, but it was discovered later that it was actually someone else who had died, he had fulfilled his duty of "keria." But if he had rent his garment for someone else and it was actually the parent who had died, he must rend again.[15]

This distinction is made also in the mending of a rent garment. For all deceased persons with the exception of parents, the rent is sewn together with large basting stitches after Shivah and then completely reunited after Shloshim. With parents, however, the stitching is done after Shloshim, and the two pieces are never to be completely reunited.[16] This is also to be observed in the case of "Delayed News," a term indicating that the bereaved has not heard of the death of the loved object until thirty full days have elapsed since burial. In such a case mourning need not be observed for more than one hour, and "keria" is not obligatory since it is not carried out with the observance of the seven days of mourning. However, "in the case of father or mother one always rends one's garment" because of the "deference to be shown." [17]

These laws which are required especially of a bereaved offspring suggest recognition by the Rabbis not only of the greater degree of libidinal attachment to a parent, but also the greater intensity of guilt feelings. The meticulous fulfillment of the various laws and rituals is a way of alleviating the guilt and appeasing the punitive superego.

Behavior Patterns in Grief. The immediate effect of the death of a loved object is shock or trauma. The two sources of this shock are frustrated emotional energy and guilt feelings. In addition, every aspect of the life of the bereaved was involved with the life of the deceased. Death, therefore, necessitates new adjustments. When death occurs, "the whole pattern of life is upset. The confusion . . . puts the mourner somewhat out of touch with reality. He is in a daze, apparently lost, even amid familiar surroundings." [18] This feeling results from the sudden disorganization of old patterns in life and is a common reaction among the bereaved in the earliest stages of grief. The first few hours, the first day or two, after the death occurs are characterized by shock and bewilderment as well as by other feelings we commonly associate with grief.

Judaism recognizes this immediate state of bewilderment in the very word applied to the bereaved during the period from death to burial. The root of this word, "anan," means to be fatigued, tired, weary as well as in great sorrow and trouble. Another related root word, "oon," means to complain. The term used for a mourner during this brief period between death and burial is "Onen," which is derived from both roots. The bereaved does not know how to react to the shock of death; there are no formed patterns for this state of emergency. The immediate reaction is one of emotional paralysis and bewilderment, coupled with inability to accept the death. Another common reaction which the Hebrew word "oon" expresses is that of resentment. The bereaved may unconsciously feel resentful that the loved object through death has caused so much anguish and pain. This feeling may easily turn into guilt since it is considered unacceptable by the superego.

Judaism thus differentiates the immediate reaction to the bereavement from that felt after the death is accepted and the shock has subsided. Therefore, the brief period of "Aninut" (from death to burial) is treated differently from "Avelut" (the entire period of mourning subsequent to burial). This difference was explicitly recognized by Rav Ashi in the Talmud.[19]

The Rabbis also realized that grief is most intense during the first few days after the death. This is brought out in a discussion in the Talmud of the number of days after a death that the mourner is forbidden to wear his "tefillin" (the phylacteries worn during morning prayers) because of the intensity of grief immediately after suffering bereavement. Rabbi Eliezer expressed the opinion that the mourner is not allowed to wear the tefillin for the first three days. But Rabbi Joshua expressed the view that a mourner is forbidden for the first two days only. But usually, others say, the "poignancy of the bitterness is but on one day." The final conclusion is that the wearing of tefillin is forbidden only for the day of burial, thus implying that intense grief in normal situations is strongest on the day of burial.[20]

One reason given for the intensity of grief during Aninut is that the bereaved is especially distressed while the deceased lies before him. When the deceased is buried and out of sight, the death is more acceptable. Once the burial takes place and "throughout the whole of seven days of mourning it is incumbent on him to carry out all religious duties." [21] While the loved one is still present, it is a time of denial, and the bereaved cannot believe that the deceased is actually dead; consequently grief cannot be fully felt or expressed. Bar Kappara stated that on the third day, the mourning is "at its height," [22] demonstrating awareness that the bereaved person gradually feels the loss of the deceased, the shock of which is at first not fully comprehended. Only after a day or two elapses does the bereaved realize the depth of the loss he has experienced.

Because of his state of shock and bewilderment, the "Onen" is exempt from fulfilling all Biblical laws during this period. He does not have to recite the blessings before and after meals. He cannot eat meat or drink wine.[23]

Thus we see that the Rabbis, in developing the laws and rituals, recognized the impact of the traumatic situation involved in immediate grief.

Abnormal Reactions. The Rabbis also realized that the traumatic state is normal during the period of Aninut, immediately after death. But Aninut (immediate grief) should not be extended for too long a period of time, and the state of shock and bewilderment should soon terminate. Extension beyond the fixed period is considered to be "unreasonable" and can only be terminated "by a protracted period." [24]

The Rabbis also were aware that grief can be abnormally excessive and may then reveal a perverted clinging to the dead:

"Weep not for the dead, neither bemoan him;" that means, "Weep not for the dead" in excess, "neither bemoan him" beyond measure. How is that (applied)? Three days for weeping and seven for lamenting and thirty (to refrain) from cutting the hair and

(donning) pressed clothes. Hereafter, the Holy One, blessed be He, says: "You are not more compassionate towards him (the departed) than I am." [25]

The philosopher Philo interpreted the Biblical narrative of the death of Sarah by concluding that Abraham did not mourn for a long period because it is not fitting for intelligent people to do so:

> . . . *after weeping for a little over the corpse he quickly arose from it, holding further mourning, it appears, to be out of keeping with wisdom. . . . And, as no reasonable person would chafe at repaying a debt or deposit to him who had proffered it, so too he must not fret when nature took back her own, but accept the inevitable with equanimity.*[26]

The Rabbis not only realized that grief could be excessive but also attempted to analyze the reason for it: "Whoever indulges in grief to excess over his dead will weep for another." [27] In other words, excessive grief could arise because the bereaved experienced an unsatisfactory grief-response to someone else who died previously. He may have experienced anticipatory or delayed grief, and was incapable of expressing his genuine feelings completely. Now that he encounters a new grief situation, the stopped-up feelings of the previous bereavement gush forth in addition to the grief-response of the present bereavement. This "doubled" grief may result in further distorted expression, and consequently the bereaved may again experience a frustrated process of mourning.

Instead of expressing himself outwardly to an excessive degree, we have already seen that the bereaved person may draw into himself and refuse to face other people or the reality of the bereavement.

> *There is commonly a slight sense of unreality, a feeling of increased emotional distance from other people (sometimes they appear shadowy or small), and there is intense preoccupation with the image of the deceased.*[28]

These characteristics, as we have seen, are considered normal during the period of Aninut and perhaps for a short time thereafter. But if protracted, then the grief may be termed abnormal. Freud considered these immediate effects of bereavement to be similar to a neurosis, but not identical with neurosis because normally these symptoms do not last.[29]

The difficulty of facing reality in the early stages of grief because the bereaved still finds it hard to accept the death of the loved one, is brought out frequently in the dreams of the bereaved, which reveal a compromise between wanting the deceased to live and realizing he is really dead.

> *Sometimes the deceased is dreamt of as being dead, and yet still alive because he does not know that he is dead, as if he would only really die if he did not know it; at other times he is half dead and half alive. . . .*[30]

The conflict between denying and accepting the reality of the loss is one of the central problems of grief. Excessive concern with the deceased and with one's own grief causes a withdrawal from reality. The bereaved is concerned with himself and with his painful feelings resulting from the death of the loved one. He may be overly concerned as a means of assuaging painful feelings of guilt or because his relationships with reality were severely limited to the deceased and to activities pertaining to the deceased. In such cases, once the loved object no longer exists the bereaved's path to the outside world is, so to speak, cut off. There is no one or nothing else to relate to besides himself or his little world, where the dead still lives. Whatever the specific reason, it is common for the bereaved to become egocentric during the initial phase of the mourning period. "Just as lovers cannot believe that any love compares with theirs, the bereaved cannot believe that any other grief compares with his." [31]

Judaism encourages the bereaved to return to reality and relate to others from the very beginning of Avelut, implying that the characteristics of egocentricity and withdrawal are abnormal. They are allowed for during Aninut, but not during Avelut. It is stated in the Letter of Aristeas that "all men do grieve, thinking only of themselves and their own interests." [32] Such preoccupation prevents the bereaved from establishing new relationships and adjusting to the new situation in life without the lost loved one.

Conclusion. Jewish sources reveal an awareness of the depth of feeling experienced in the grief situation. The loss of a loved object is recognized as extremely painful and disrupting.

The depth of the grief-response depends on the intensity of the interaction between bereaved and deceased prior to death. This is in accord with the investment of libidinal energy and the frustration of this energy as a result of the death of the loved one. There is an especially intense relationship between parent and offspring due to several dynamic factors discussed.

Judaism recognizes that the pain of separation is most intense during the first few days after the death, especially during the brief period of Aninut (before burial) when the bereaved experiences shock and bewilderment due to the difficulty of fully accepting the loss. Because the life of the bereaved is so intimately interwoven with that of the deceased, he experiences great difficulty also in relating to anyone or anything else after the death. This inability to relate to reality may be normal at first, but if it is protracted Judaism considers it to be a distorted reaction to bereavement. Excessive grief can be the result of causes other than the loss of the loved object itself. If both excessive grief and withdrawal continue for a long period, the process of mourning may be severely obstructed.

1. See Lindemann, *op. cit.*, pp. 146–147; also. Paul E. Irion, *The Funeral and the Mourners* (New York and Nashville: Abingdon Press, 1954), p. 31.

2. MK 21b.

3. KSA, 203:2.

4. Sem. 11:11; CHL, p. 339, note 11.

5. CHL, p. 287, note 32.

6. Ta'anit 13b.

7. SA, YD 396:3.

8. MK 24b.

9. BM 18a; Sem. 4:3.

10. See Amos 8:10; Jeremiah 6:26; Zechariah 12:10.

11. MK 22a–22b.

12. MK 26b.

13. MK 22b; Sem. 9:10–13; SA, YD 390:4.

14. MK 22b.

15. Sem. 9:4.

16. MK 22b; Sem. 9:4, 6–8.

17. MK 20b.

18. Irion, *op. cit.*, p. 46; See Waller and Hill, *op. cit.*, p. 478; Jackson, *op. cit.*, p. 187.

19. Yeb. 43B; see also Maimonides's *Hilchot Avel* 1:2.

20. MK 21a; SA, YD 388:1.

21. Deut. R., 9:1; see also Zeb 100b (p. 483); Sem. 4:4; Lev. R., 18:1; Eccl. R., 12:6.

22. Gen. R., 100:7; cf. Folkman, *op. cit.*, pp. 5–6.

23. M. Ber. 3:1; SA, YD 341:1; MK 3b; Sem. 101–2. The Onen must, of course, continue to observe all negative commandments ("Thou shalt not . . .").

24. Gen. R. 64:5.

25. MK 27b.

26. "On Abraham", trans. F. H. Colson ("The Loeb Classical Library", Vol. VI; Cambridge: Harvard University Press, 1935), p. 127 (No. 44). Cf. the story concerning the loss of the two sons of Meir and Beruriah in Midrash Proverbs 30:10.

27. MK 27b; SA, YD 394:1.

28. Lindemann, *op. cit.*, p. 142.

29. Freud, *A General Introduction to Psychoanalysis*, p. 287.

30. *Ibid.*, pp. 196–197; see Waller and Hill, *op. cit.*, p. 476; these authors speculate that resurrection legends may have grown out of bereavement dreams in which the deceased appears to be alternately alive and dead (p. 477).

31. Folkman, *op. cit.*, p. 22.

32. *Aristeas to Philocrates*, ed. and trans. Moses Hadas (New York: Harper & Brothers, 1951), p. 205 (No. 268). A similar statement is, "All go to the house of mourning and each one weeps over his own sorrow (Ibn Shuaib, Olat Shabbat 53)."

IV

Ambivalence and Guilt

Introduction. We have seen in Chapter I that ambivalence is a natural phenomenon of the psyche, derived from the two instincts of love and hate. These feelings in turn give rise to feelings of guilt since the superego (or conscience) punishes the bereaved for experiencing contradictory feelings towards the dead. The punishment of the ego for its aggressive impulses accounts for one of the two sources of anxiety characteristic of bereavement behavior. The other is the loss of love and the consequent frustration of libidinal energy. Judaism recognizes this frustration and loss of love as a result of permanent separation from the deceased. Therapeutic techniques developed for handling grief cannot possibly be effective if they do not account for these deep-seated factors.

Do the legal and cultural sources of Judaism cope with ambivalence as a primary cause of the profound suffering experienced by the bereaved? Is there indication in Jewish sources that guilt feelings are understood to be a result of ambivalence?

General Cultural Considerations. Feelings of ambivalence are universal, not only in the experience of every human being individually, but also in most cultures generally. Freud has stated that "the same feeling of ambivalence is responsible for the fact that the dreamer, the child, and the savage all have the same attitude towards the dead." [1] The formal usages relative to death and mourning by primitive cultures usually express ambivalent attitudes towards the deceased. Some rites appear to encourage complete severance from the deceased, while others assume that the bereaved may display his affection for the deceased and desire to maintain a relationship with him, even though he is dead, and he with the bereaved.

In all primitive cultures there are taboos when a death occurs. The bereaved relatives are in a state of taboo, and are prevented from engaging in certain activities. "The taboo prohibition is to be explained as the result of an emotional ambivalence." [2] They express the need to mourn, through their prohibitory character and, at the same time, serve the purpose of hiding feelings of hostility toward the dead experienced by the bereaved relative.

The deceased is also taboo, in the sense that while his body is attended, it is also shunned and rejected. The rites of various primitive cultures display this ambivalence—a desire to get rid of the deceased and at the same time an unwillingness to let him go. [3] For example, in ancient Egyptian culture the corpse was mummified for preservation and given food and utensils, but also buried and put out of the way. It is alive and also dead. Mandelbaum gives an example of the same practice among the Apache Indians in North America: "There is a period when it is proper for mourners to give vent to their grief. . . . At other times, the name and memory of a dead person must be expunged from recall and remembrance." [4]

The individual conscience or superego is developed not only from parental influences but also from the authority of the group. The development of rites and customs to express ambivalence serves the purpose of meeting a basic emotional conflict within the bereaved individual, which might engender guilt feelings. If the group value conflicts with the individual value, a heightened sense of guilt might be the consequence; hence, the culture provides an outlet for the natural feelings of ambivalence. The individual internalizes the opposing authority of the culture as part of his superego, which might resort to punitive measures against him if it is in opposition to his feelings of ambivalence.

The expression of ambivalence is not allowed to develop within every culture. But when it is, the bereaved individual's opportunity for attaining emotional stability after the death of a loved object is that much greater.

Burial and Memorial. Jewish culture also reflects the same ambivalence as in other cultures between the desire to hold on to the dead and the desire to get rid of him. Although disposing of the corpse as soon as possible, it has mourning ceremonies which guarantee the perpetuation of the dead. Fear and the defense of projection are involved in this.

Jewish law required that burial should take place on the very day of death. It was uncommon for the body to be kept until the next day. Precautions were taken not only to bury the body as quickly as possible, but also to make sure that once buried it was covered over securely. Once the body was lowered, the grave had to be filled very quickly so that the body would not be exposed long. Tombstones afforded even greater surety that the body would remain where it was placed and never "bother" the living. "Among some peoples the custom prevailed of even piling a mass of heavy stones on the grave." [5]

In Biblical times, also, hasty burials were commonly practiced. The book of Deuteronomy states that the body of a criminal could not be left exposed overnight, but had to be buried on the day of death. The reason given is that "a body left hanging brings down the curse of God." This did not apply only to criminals. The Bible also states that because the bones of Saul and Jonathan were left unburied, the Israelites suffered calamity which did not cease until the bones were buried.[6] In other cultures of the time, such as Babylonia and Assyria, the same feeling is expressed towards the unburied body. Delayed burial is considered not merely a curse to the dead but also a danger to the living.[7]

The injunction to bury promptly is expressed not only in Biblical law but also in Rabbinic law, which states that the person who hastens the burial of the dead is actually praiseworthy. However, the person who expedites the burial of his mother or father is blameworthy.[8] This enactment is no doubt an expression of ambivalence, the motive behind it being to allay guilt. Because the relationship between parent and offspring is so sensitive, great care was taken in Jewish law to protect the feelings of the survivors, which were assumed to be so powerful towards the deceased that even the legal enactments were subjugated to them. Hence, out of deference to parents the law allowed for the utmost leniency to display affection and attention. With other relatives prompt burial was required. Hastening the burial of parents would constitute too quickly an acceptance of the death; postponement reveals the desire of the offspring to keep alive and preserve the memory of the dead parent. Thus, in the case of a deceased parent, the love-aspect predominates over the hate-aspect.

There was another purpose to burial itself besides that of disposing of the corpse. It was believed that the process of bodily decay in the grave was painful to the deceased. This afforded the deceased a means of atonement for the sins he committed while he was alive. Below the surface, the bereaved thinks atonement was required because of the sins the deceased committed in life against the bereaved. By feeling that the deceased deserves to decay and to feel pain because of his sins, one gains an acceptable way of expressing aggression. This view of atonement "induced some to bring the body into close contact with the earth by either having the coffin perforated or by dispensing with the coffin altogether," thereby expediting the decomposition of the body.[9]

When the body is cared for immediately after death and is treated as far as is consonant with Jewish law to prevent deterioration, it expresses the opposite position toward the deceased than is evident in hasty burial. The Talmud records some disagreement concerning the ointments most effective for preserving the body. Akiba stated that wine and oil should be sprinkled on the body, but Simeon bar

Nanos objected to wine because it causes deterioration. "And the sages said: 'Neither oil nor wine because they breed wood-worms, but we place dry clods of earth upon them.' " [10] The body is treated carefully and gently, yet it is buried as soon as possible.

The erection of tombstones is not a legal requirement, yet it was and still is a common custom. They are usually erected after a twelve-month period. The reason given is "that the dead should not be forgotten." [11] Tombstones are mentioned even in Biblical times, and specifications for tombs are given in the Mishna.[12]

During Mishnaic times the custom prevailed of gathering together the bones of the deceased after about a year from the rock-sepulchre where the body was placed originally, and placing them in an ossuary, which was a small casket made of stone. The gathering of bones is considered by Rabbi Meir, in the Mishna, to be "an occasion for rejoicing" while Rabbi Jose considers it "an occasion for mourning." [13] This disagreement symbolizes the ambivalent character of the custom. To Meir, the ceremony marks the end of the relationship between deceased and bereaved, and symbolizes complete riddance from the deceased. But to Rabbi Jose this is not a final severance although it is a sorrowful occasion. Rabbi Jose's view is confirmed by the specifications as to the method of gathering the bones:

> *The bones of two corpses may be gathered at the same time. The one may be placed at one end of the sheet and the other at the opposite end, according to Rabbi Akiba. Rabbi Johanan ben Buri said: With this method, the sheet may ultimately decay and the bones*

will be mixed; therefore, we should place them sepa-
rately in cedar boxes.[14]

The ceremony serves to get rid of the remains of the corpse permanently, but also to preserve the individual identity of the deceased.

That this ceremony is held to be an occasion of sorrow, despite Meir's view, is confirmed in the statement that the bereaved who gathers the bones of a parent "holds himself in mourning for them all the day." [15] This stipulation gives more expression in law and ceremony to affection and love for a parent than to feelings of hostility, and is similar to the considerations connected with postponing the burial of a parent. The rending of the garments (keria) again at the time of gathering the bones is another expression of the sorrow of the occasion.[16] This was performed by the same bereaved persons who tore their garments at the time of death.

In its ceremonies of burial and memorial, the Jewish culture fulfills the deep human need for expression of the contradictory tendencies to feel aggression and love at the same time.

The Mourner's Meal. The ceremony relating to the first meal served to the mourners after the burial expresses the ambivalence of the bereaved. This ceremony originated in Biblical times and is mentioned in regard to those who came to break bread with David after his loss of Abner. Jeremiah also mentions the breaking of bread for those in mourning.[17] Bread was the most common type of food represented at the repast for mourners, as mentioned also in other Biblical passages.[18] The custom of eating bread extended into post-Biblical times. A midrashic passage states that a woman went to comfort her neighbor who was in mourning and brought her "two round loaves." [19] The post-Talmudic literature also states that "the main part of the mourner's meal is the bread. . . ." [20]

Bread has always served as an important symbol in many belief-systems. It is often regarded as possessing supernatural qualities; sometimes it is regarded in the supernatural as the body itself. The Aztecs, for example, baked cakes twice yearly in the form of one of their idols, and then ate the cakes. In the Church, the familiar practice of eating the bread symbolizes partaking of the body of Jesus. In Judaism, bread did not actually symbolize the body or image of God, but it still possessed supernatural qualities, and represented the departed person. Once dead the deceased was considered supernatural, being no longer among the living, and the eating of bread, therefore, acquired a symbolic significance.

Wine also was an important part of the meal for mourners. In Jeremiah, it is called the "cup of consolation." [21] As time passed, the custom became common, and in Talmudic times ten cups of wine were drunk in the house of mourning.[22] This practice is also symbolic of consuming the dead person. Wine too was considered to have supernatural qualities, as we see expressed in the Church communion in which wine is actually or symbolically, depending on the denomination, the blood of Jesus.

Another common food eaten at the mourner's meal was lentils. The Talmud regards it as a symbol of death and mourning.[23] The egg, still another common food, represents the supernatural and the dead in the folklore of many cultures. Like lentils, the egg is round, smooth and has no openings, representing the uninterrupted continuum of death. Both, in turn, become symbols of the deceased, who is the personification of death.[24]

These dishes were provided for the mourner at the special meal after burial because it was recognized that the mourner would have great difficulty eating anything after the death of the loved object.[25] The mourner does not have to eat, if he finds it repulsive to do so. One codifier of the law says that the mourner can fast during the whole first day of Avelut, although other codifiers disagree with this opinion.[26] It is obligatory upon his neighbors to provide for the mourner the very first meal after the burial. He may eat his own food at the second meal.[27] As to the reason why the first meal must be provided by others, it is stated that there may be a refusal by the mourner to eat.[28]

Clearly, the special foods provided for the mourner all in some way represent the deceased, and the first meal is obligatory because the bereaved usually wants no food at all. It seems obvious that the ceremony of the mourner's meal was unconsciously built around the ambivalence of the bereaved, which expresses itself in the form of oral incorporation and expulsion, destroying the deceased through expulsion and taking food as an expression of incorporating him in order to preserve him. However, incorporation can also be secondarily destructive, as well as a means of holding on to the deceased through internalizing and identifying with him. The obligatory nature and the special foods consumed at the mourner's meal allow the mourner to express both the impulse to preserve through introjecting the deceased and the impulse to destroy, unconsciously expressing feelings of hostility through the same process of ingestion. The mourner's meal therefore symbolizes the double-edged attitude of bereaved individuals towards loved objects whom they have lost.

The Recognition of Guilt. The superego or conscience makes no distinction between intention and deed. When aggression is felt towards a loved object, the conscience views this as tantamount to actual aggression, which is intolerable. The superego seeks revenge by engendering guilt in the bereaved person. Judaism provides amply for expression of the ambivalence of the mourner, but feelings of guilt are so powerful and relentless that the mourner experiences them in spite of the ceremonies and laws that give vent to impulses of hostility.

Judaism recognizes that while guilt may be assuaged, it cannot be completely controlled. This is seen in a midrashic story about Jacob's grief over the supposed death of his son Joseph. The midrashic text states that Jacob grieved for another reason besides the death of Joseph itself. God had once said to Jacob that if any of his sons died during his lifetime he would be placed in Gehinnom (hell) after his death.[29] There is the intimation in this legend that Jacob's grief involves much more than a response to the death itself. It is also related to guilt stemming from his attitudes and relations to his sons. This explains his concern over being placed in Gehinnom. Parents can feel ambivalent toward children as well as children toward parents. Jacob probably thought himself an unworthy father.

In another midrashic text dealing with the same Biblical account, Jacob blames himself for the death of his son, and says:

Would God I had died for thee, O Joseph, my son,
for now I am distressed on thy account. . . . Arise,
arise from thy place, and look upon my grief for thee.
Come and count the tears that roll down my cheeks,
and bring the tale of them before God, that His wrath
be turned away from me. . . . I know well that it
(the death) came to pass by reason of my sins. . . .[30]

The same recognition of guilt can be observed in the Biblical account of David's grief for his sick child, the offspring of Bath-Sheba, who was originally the wife of Uriah, whom David had killed so that he could marry her. David said: "I have sinned against the Lord," and began to grieve, although the child was still alive. This confession of sin was prompted by his guilt for the murder of Uriah, to which he attributed the fact that the child was dying.[31]

In post-Biblical times, it was customary to ask forgiveness of the deceased at time of burial "for any offense" that the bereaved might "have committed against him." This required the presence of ten persons.[32]

In the following provision, feelings of guilt are provided for by Jewish law:

If a mourner did not observe Shivah whether intentionally or not, he is permitted to make it up during the Shloshim, except for keria. If he did not perform keria in the hour of greatest suffering, then he may rend only during the seven days, except in the case of his parents for whom he may perform keria even after the seven days.[33]

Even the person who has been intentionally neglectful is allowed, in the insightful leniency of this law, to make up for the mourning period he has missed. The Rabbis evidently realized the delicacy of feeling involved in a loss, and the variety of deep psychic factors in the mourner's reaction. The power of guilt feelings was realized in this law; the intentionally neglectful person would eventually suffer greater guilt than the unintentionally neglectful. This law also realized that the guilt feelings experienced by a bereaved offspring are greater than any others; hence it provides for keria (the tearing of garments) even after Shivah. Even delayed performance of the various mourning rites causes the suffering of guilt to be allayed to some extent.

The same reasoning is evident in the law of "Delayed News," discussed earlier.[34] If news of the death is not received until after thirty days from the day of burial, then the act of mourning that must be performed need only fulfill the requirements of the Shloshim. In this way, the law removes the guilt the mourner feels at not having honored the dead sooner, by fulfilling all the mourning rites. If news of the death is received during the first thirty days ("Timely News"), the bereaved must fulfill the requirements of Shivah. If there are any days remaining after Shivah, they are observed as part of Shloshim. In any case, the "delayed" provisions of the law set up a lenient procedure to allay the mourner's feelings of guilt. The "timely" provisions afford the mourner an opportunity to assuage his feelings of guilt by performing all the requirements of regular mourning.[35]

We see, thus, that Judaism is sensitive to the painfulness of the mourner's feelings.

Conclusion. Burial of the body is a practical way of disposing of the dead, but the ambivalence related to such customs as the mourner's meal affords us a clue to its double meaning. The bereaved derives comfort from the company of other people and allays guilt feelings through ceremonials and rituals.

There may be several motivations involved in a specific law or ritual. It is helpful to understand the fundamental psychodynamic factors, which are at the root of the law, ceremony or legend related to mourning customs and which illuminate reasons for their existence. By delving deeper into the human psyche we may learn which is the "truest" interpretation.

We have seen that Judaism takes account of the ambivalence of the bereaved person and the consequent guilt feelings that he experiences; also that the two basic impulses which produce the severity of grief are frustration of love impulses and ambivalent feelings in the bereaved.

1. Freud, *Totem and Taboo*, p. 855.

2. *Ibid.*, p. 859.

3. Jackson, *op. cit.*, p. 90; W. Robertson Smith, *The Religion of the Semites* (New York: Meridian Books, 1957), p. 336, note 2; E. Sidney Hartland, "Death and Disposal of the Dead (Introductory), "Encyclopedia of Religion and Ethics, ed. James Hastings IV (1911), 426; Bronislaw Malinowski, *Magic, Science and Religion* (Garden City, New York: Doubleday Anchor Books, 1954), p. 49.

4. David G. Mandelbaum, "Social Uses of Funeral Rites," *The Meaning of Death*, ed. Herman Feifel (New York: McGraw-Hill Book Company, Inc., 1959), p. 207.

5. Schauss, *op. cit.*, p. 288; Joshua Trachtenberg, *Jewish Magic and Superstition* (New York: Behrman's Jewish Book House, 1939), p. 49; Solomon Freehof, *Reform Jewish Practice* (Cincinnati: Hebrew Union College Press, 1952), II, 106.

6. Deut. 21:23; I Samuel 31, II Samuel 21.

7. Moses Buttenweiser, "Blood Revenge and Burial Rites in Ancient Israel," *JAOS*, Vol. 39, Part V (1912), pp. 312–313.

8. MK 22a; see also San. 47a and SA, YD 403:1.

9. "Burial," *Jewish Encyclopedia*, III, p. 432.

10. Sem. 12:9.

11. KSA 199:17.

12. Gen. 35:20; M.BB 6:8; also, M.MK 1:6.

13. M.MK 1:5.

14. Sem. 12:8; SA, YD 403:8.

15. MK 8a; Sem. 12:4; SA, YD 403:1.

16. Sem. 12:3; SA, YD 403:2. See the following for comparable ceremonies in other cultures: James G. Frazer, *The Belief in Immortality and the Worship of the Dead* (London: Macmillan and Co., Limited, 1913), pp. 225, 294, 328.

17. II Sam. 3:35; Jer. 16:7; see also Lam. R. 4:13. The custom of a second burial was confined to Palestine during the Greco-Roman period (see Schauss, *op. cit.*, p. 244).

18. Hosea 9:4; Ezek. 24:17.

19. Lev. R. 6:3.

20. CHL, p. 250, note 1.

21. Jer. 16:7.

22. Sem. 14:14; see also "Pirke de Rabbi Eliezer," trans. Gerald Friedlander (London: Kegan Paul, Trench, Trubner & Co. Ltd., 1916), p. 117.

23. BB 16b; SA, YD 378:9; Ginzberg, *op. cit.*, I, 319.

24. *Funk & Wagnalls Standard Dictionary of Folklore, Mythology and Legend*, ed. Maria Leach, I (1949), 162, 341.

25. CHL, p. 250, note 1 ("according to Perisha").

26. SA, YD 378:3.

27. SA, YD 378:1.

28. CHL, p. 250, note 1 (according to "Perisha"). See the following for comparable examples of the Mourner's Meal: Frazer, *op. cit.*, I, 184ff.; Effie Bendann, *Death Customs: An Analytical Study of Burial Rites* ("The History of Civilization," ed. C. K. Ogden; New York: Alfred A. Knopf, 1930), pp. 149ff.; Smith, *op. cit.*, pp. 322–323; Malinowski, *op. cit.*, p. 50; Hartland, *op. cit.*, pp. 435–436.

29. Rashi's commentary to Genesis 37:35.

30. *Ibid.*, 26, based on Yashar Va-Yeshev, 84a–84b.

31. II Sam. 12:15–23.

32. Joshua S. Sperka, *Eternal Life: A Digest of all Laws of Mourning* (New York: Bloch Publishing Co., Inc., 1939), p. 136; "Dead, Duty to the," *Jewish Encyclopedia*, IV, p. 477.

33. SA, YD 396:1.

34. *Supra*, p. 41.

35. Pes. 4a; Erub. 46a; MK 20a; Gen. R., 100:7; SA, YD 402:1–2.

V

Symbols of Defense

Introduction. The pain of anxiety, as we have shown, accounts for the severity of grief felt and expressed by the bereaved individual. Judaism, in its legal expression and cultural modes, accounts for the sources of anxiety and provides outlets in mourning customs for its pervasiveness in the grief situation.

The ego enlists defenses to protect itself from the trauma of deep emotional conflicts giving rise to anxiety. These defenses are not always entirely satisfying, but tend only to disguise the deepest feelings of the psyche. They are convenient and expedient but not emotionally sound. The most important defense and usually the one initially utilized is that of repression. Because it is not always effective as a method of getting rid of the pain, the ego turns to other defenses. In the Jewish sources, repression is also posited as the basic and initial defense, and the entire mourning procedure of Judaism is a countermeasure calculated to overcome the mechanism of repression. However, the defenses, especially repression, have great force, and the adjustive provisions do not necessarily overcome the ego's compulsion to employ them. If there is even a partial failure to do so, the development of the other defenses may be unavoidable. In the Jewish sources, the assumption is that the defenses of repression, regression, and denial are not actually encouraged, but are to be avoided for the emotional welfare of the mourner.

How, in Jewish sources, is the mourner's need to utilize the two defenses of self-punishment and projection accounted for?

Self-Punishment. The bereaved person inflicts punishment on himself "in order to diminish the sense of guilt." In so doing, he "saves himself from some of the severity of internal (self-) punishment." [1] This mechanism of defense receives expression almost immediately after the death of a loved object in the Onen. During the period of Aninut, while others are reading the "Tefillah" (the nineteen benedictions which are part of the traditional Jewish liturgy), he is supposed to recite the following prayer:

> *Master of the Universe, I have sinned before Thee. I have fulfilled few responsibilities and I deserve much more punishment than this. May it be Thy will to unite and comfort us.* [2]

The prayer is, in one sense, a confession of guilt; but even more it expresses the hope that more punishment will be inflicted upon the bereaved. This hope in itself may help to alleviate the severity of the mourner's guilt feelings. In the Bible, a similar kind of hope is expressed by David in connection with the death of his son Absalom, that he might have died instead. This desire may of course have arisen unconsciously as a means of allaying David's strong sense of guilt. David probably felt neglected and even hostile toward Absalom because of his rebelliousness. After Absalom's death, he felt the need to punish himself by expressing suicidal wishes.[3]

An extreme form of this desire for punishment is self-mutilation. This is a common practice among many peoples throughout the world, and is displayed in a variety of bizarre ways. In some places the mourners cut their heads open as they stand by the open grave. In other places they may sever fingers or toes, or burn their breasts and faces.[4] In most of these cultures satisfaction is not really obtained until the blood of the mourner is visible.

There is ample evidence that self-mutilation was a common practice during Biblical times, even though the practices may not have been as extreme. The commandment which follows bears this out: "Ye shall not make any cuttings in your flesh for the dead, nor imprint any marks upon you." [5] The fact that it is a legal prohibition justifies the inference that it was not only practiced, but was perhaps a popular practice.

That the practice extended into the Rabbinic period is indicated by similar legislation in the Mishna: "If a man . . . made any cuttings for the dead, he is liable (to the Forty Stripes)." [6] The law is repeated even in the Shulchan Aruch, although by the middle ages and onwards there was probably very little self-mutilation among Jews.[7]

However, earlier, during the first centuries of the Common Era in spite of the legal prohibition, self-mutilation was actually practiced in moderate degree. There is an account of Rabbi Akiba's reaction to the death of his colleague, Rabbi Eliezer:

After the Sabbath Rabbi Akiba came upon (his remains) being carried on the highway leading from Caesarea to Lydda. Forthwith he rent his clothes and tore at his heart—and his blood ran down to the ground. . . .[8]

In another account we learn that Rabbi Zeira, when he was in mourning, fell to the ground in order "to afflict himself."[9] Some form of physical infliction was evidently condoned. The custom is practiced infrequently in modern times, although Schauss reports, "the Moroccan Jews still scratch and cut their faces as a sign of mourning, notwithstanding their rabbis' denunciation of the practice as a flagrant transgression of the Mosaic law."[10]

Because Jewish law was so vehemently opposed to physical infliction, the practice of keria was developed as a substitute in order to satisfy the mourner's need to punish himself. The methods of fulfilling keria are "a later form of the more primitive practice,[11] and are analogous to tearing one's flesh or hair. The Biblical statement is, "rend your heart and not your garments."[12] Keria became such a popular substitute for the practice of self-mutilation even in Biblical times, that the ceremony itself developed all out of proportion.

Keria, according to Jewish law, should be performed at a time when the bereaved is most inclined to afflict himself physically. It should be done "at the moment of greatest suffering."[13] The emotional intensity accompanying the act is confirmed by the literal meaning of the word which, according to Jastrow, is "a violent action of tearing." [14]

The popularity of sublimated forms of self-mutilation is shown by the substitutes of which keria was one, common in Biblical times. The way clothes were taken off the body, by tearing them off violently, suggests a form of keria.[15] As society became more conscious of social refinements, this custom was altered to partial nakedness, exposing only a portion of the body—arms, shoulders or feet. The baring of the shoulders is considered legally optional, although for parents it is a requirement. The same is true of baring the chest by means of keria.[16]

The most common sublimated substitute for total nakedness became baring of the feet. While it is a Talmudic dictum, its origins are to be found in Biblical times.[17] The mourners are supposed to remove their shoes or sandals immediately after the grave is covered with earth.[18] This practice was later modified by allowing the mourner to keep his shoes on if they are not made of leather.[19] It was also a custom that the pallbearers were to walk barefoot with the bier, a further development in social refinement, but this was applicable only in Talmudic times.[20]

All these practices are sublimated forms for physical mutilation, which is the extreme expression of self-punishment. However, the need to punish oneself can be expressed in many ways besides physical violence, such as various forms of self-denial or abstention, like abstention from certain kinds of foods or partial or total fasting. These also serve the purpose of alleviating the sense of guilt. Such forms of self-denial have been practiced since Biblical times. The Bible mentions that mourners may eat the hallowed food which is tithed in the year of tithing.[21] Since the Rabbinic period, the Onen has been required to abstain from meat and wine. When the deceased is a mother or a father, the mourner is expected to fast completely on the day of the death.[22]

Another common practice is to consume whatever food may be eaten away from the "sight" of the corpse.[23] This custom arose out of the belief that the mourner should not show the deceased that he is concerned at all with his own welfare at such a time.

Another common practice is for the mourners to sit on low stools throughout the period of Shivah. The original version of this custom was to overturn all chairs and beds in the house and sit on the ground throughout the seven days. The Biblical reason given for this custom is self-humiliation which is, of course, in line with the interpretation that these observances are all forms of self-punishment.[24] A similar form of self-humiliation observed in the Biblical period was rolling in ashes, dirt and dust.[25] The Talmud also bears this out in a statement that the mourner should be uncomfortable because of his sins.[26] The feeling of sin is connected with the sense of guilt, which in turn leads to the need to punish or deny oneself.

In line with the prohibition of all forms of pleasurable experience, the wearing of attractive apparel was also discouraged. This applied especially to female mourners, who are presumed to be more conscious of sartorial appeal. It is stated that a woman should remove all jewelry or adornment "so she should sit and be seen in a disheveled condition."[27] In fact, one of the Hebrew words used for mourning, "kadar," means to be dark or dirty and gloomy in appearance.[28] To achieve this gloomy appearance, black was most frequently worn by the mourner.

During Biblical times it was common to wear sackcloth as a sign of mourning. Sackcloth is coarse and rough, and irritating to the skin. It therefore served two purposes: it was a mild form of physical punishment, as well as being ugly in appearance. Sackcloth was also worn by slaves, making it a type of clothing conferring inferior status on others. This custom did not persist beyond Biblical times. From the beginning of the Common Era, sartorial factors in mourning customs among Jews have varied considerably, depending largely on the local environments in which Jews have settled.[29]

Cutting the hair was originally a substitute form of self-mutilation, similar to keria. It was, however, prohibited according to both Biblical and Rabbinic law, along with all other types of self-mutilation.[30] In the Rabbinic law, the very opposite actually became the rule: that the hair must remain uncut for the entire period of Shloshim.[31] The Rabbinic law was not in line with the taboo against self-mutilation, but was more likely established because going with uncut hair is taken to be a form of self-humiliation. An ugly appearance became a characteristic of mourning since it is an effective way of punishing oneself. For one, it induces a feeling of shame in the mourner to appear unkempt before others. Moreover, it made him look distressed, proving that he could not give attention to anything regarding himself or his appearance during the mourning period. The same rationale applied to the action of letting the fingernails grow.[32]

This lack of concern with appearance or one's welfare expressed itself in other abstentions, as in not bathing or wearing new or pressed clothes, and not indulging in sexual intercourse. The mourner cannot study or work either, unless great loss might be suffered.[33] All these relatively innocuous vehicles of abstention, self-humiliation, and mild self-punishment are the substitue forms that Judaism developed to sublimate the impulse of self-mutilation, which it wished to counteract.

The Fear Motive. Aggressive impulses and hostility directed against the deceased cannot be tolerated by the bereaved. The superego turns against the ego and punishes it for harboring such impulses and, as a consequence of the engendered guilt, the ego may direct even more punitive measures against itself. Another unconscious defense process employed is to project the hostility onto the deceased. This creates the feeling in the bereaved that it is the deceased who harbors the hostility and who feels aggressive.

As Irion points out:

> *It is entirely possible in some cases that the deceased is feared as well as mourned. In our sophisticated society we are beyond the superstitious belief in haunting spirits which must be placated with ritualistic observances. Any fear of the dead which would be found in modern man would be largely, if not completely, unconscious. But this does not make it any less real.*[34]

It is difficult for modern sophisticated man to believe consciously that the deceased actually has any thoughts at all or feels any aggressive impulses. However, the Unconscious operates differently; within it this mechanism of projection can work effectively and, as a result, the bereaved may unconsciously fear the dead.

In ancient civilizations and less sophisticated societies, the belief that the dead could think and feel was quite prevalent. Many mourning customs which originated in early periods of history are based on the fear motive—fear and dread of the corpse. To quote Bendann,

> *There seems no other conclusion to come to in regard to the various attentions bestowed upon the dead of all ancient and primitive peoples than the view of Frazer, who says that they sprang not so much from the affections as from the fears of the survivors. "It is the way of all ghosts from Britanny to Samoa."* [35]

In modern society, the same defense mechanism as is unconsciously at work within less sophisticated individuals may take such forms as lavish funerals, eulogies of disproportionate praise, and costly memorials. In the unsophisticated society, it is due to belief in ghosts and spirits. But in modern society, fear and dread lead to different means of appeasing the dead and reducing the hostility supposedly felt by the deceased. The feeling of fear, whether ancient or modern, when it develops in a mourner, stems from unconscious ideas about what the hostile ghost may do to the living.[36]

The word "fear" is used in this context instead of "anxiety" since the latter refers to a more diffuse feeling arising out of the Unconscious, which is experienced by the bereaved. The person who experiences anxiety does not usually know why he feels such profound apprehension and physical discomfort, but on the other hand, the source of fear is usually known to the person experiencing it. In the case of bereavement, it is the dead person who is feared. One difference then between anxiety and fear is that of cognition, and another is the emotional sensations which arise. If there are no rituals and ceremonies which serve the purpose of appeasing the dead, fear can turn into anxiety, and the bereaved may come to feel, or feel the victim of, overwhelming hostility.

Thus, the defense of projection is seen to be an unsatisfactory one. It arises to protect the ego from the painful state of anxiety, but it is not uncommon for it eventually to develop into an attitude of fear, which is almost as painful to the bereaved as anxiety. There are more satisfactory ways to handle fear than anxiety. Superstitions which develop from belief in the activities of the dead are regarded as an unwholesome process by Jewish authorities. From earliest times they were opposed to all superstitions and beliefs connected with ghosts and spirits. Although the mechanism of projection was not known, their position was, in a sense, that of protesting against this type of reaction.

In Biblical times people believed in ghosts, but protests were made against such belief.[37] In spite of this opposition, mention of demons and ghosts is not uncommon in Jewish folklore. "They can assume any shape that they wish, they know the future, and they can move about freely. . . . Above all, they can see living people without being seen by them."[38] This last belief reflects the impact that projection makes on the psyche.

In the Jewish polypsychism of the middle ages, it was believed that the human being possessed several spirits. The "neshamah" went to heaven immediately after burial, but the "nefesh" stayed behind for about a year, visiting the grave and yearning for the body it once inhabited. It is the "nefesh" that is especially feared since it can become angry if provoked by the living and may be inclined to do harm. One method used for avoiding this harm was exorcism, and the following formula could be recited:

With the consent of the celestial and earthly tribunals, I conjure you in the name of the God of heaven and earth, and by all the holy Names, that you desist from pursuing any human. . . . and that you do them no harm with your body or your spirit or your soul.[39]

A common belief prevalent in the folklore of the Jewish people was that contact could be made between the living and the dead, although this belief never did penetrate normative, legal Judaism. The dreams of the bereaved concerning the deceased, in which the latter would try to entice the living to come away with them, very likely account for this belief to some degree. This was coupled with the belief that if the living ever yielded, his fate would be death. The dead parent would also sometimes appear in the dreams of the children and try to choke them in their sleep. As a result, the bereaved was warned to have nothing at all to do with the dead spirit.[40] A belief that the dead may be conscious reaches extremes in folklore, but it is revealed in more objective Jewish law as well. This belief is naturally accompanied by feelings of fear.

The deceased is believed to receive judgment twelve months from the day of death. During the intervening time the bereaved is expected to help the deceased by reciting

the Kaddish prayer and reading the Services. If the bereaved did not do so, the deceased would be angry and
might perhaps harm the living. It is a custom, therefore,
that a mourner must act as Reader in the synagogue on the
Sabbath during Avelut. This custom must be more strin-
gently observed during the Services at the end of the Sabbath "which is the time when the souls are returning to the
Gehena; and this is true of every evening, because the
judgment is then rigorous." [41]

It was believed that the spirits assembled at night in the
synagogue. If anyone passing by heard his own name mentioned by the spirits, it was an omen that he was certain to
die soon. The synagogue was therefore avoided at night.[42]

Some of these and other customs are based on superstitions arising largely out of the general non-Jewish environment which seemingly influenced the Jews, yet some are
reflected indigenously in the established rites and laws,
even though extreme beliefs in spirits of the dead never did
become an integral part of Judaism and was always de-
nounced by Rabbinic leaders. What did penetrate normative Judaism was modified versions of this belief. For our
purpose, it is essential to notice the various customs and
laws which utilized the defense of projection in the form of
fear and avoidance of the dead.

Fear and Mourning Customs. The attitude of fear, common in all civilizations, is based on the belief that contact
with the dead is both defiling and dangerous. One must
therefore try to avoid both the dead and anyone who has
come in contact with the dead, including the mourners and
anyone else who may have helped to prepare the corpse for
burial.[43] The Biblical term "tamé," which is translated as

"unclean," did not originally have this meaning, but is more accurately equated with "taboo." The person who was "tamé" was banned, ostracized, ritually unfit. According to Biblical law, the corpse was "tamé," but also "he that touched any man's dead body" remained "tamé" for seven days.[44] This, of course, is the origin of Shivah, the seven-day mourning period, and is probably based on fear of the dead. Since the mourners who came in contact with the corpse were taboo, it was necessary for them to remain isolated from the rest of the group. A similar belief extended into Talmudic times. There are several passages in the Talmud which place the mourner in a special class of segregation, in the same category as a leper or an excommunicant.[45]

The mourner did not, however, remain permanently "tamé" and therefore separated. In Biblical law, provisions were made for the mourner to return gradually to the group. On the third and seventh day after the death, a "clean" person would take hyssop, dip it into a vessel of ashes mixed with water and sprinkle the mixture on the "unclean" mourner.[46] Ashes, an ingredient used in soap, were, in a sense, a potion for purification. In this way, the mourner gradually reinstated himself as a member of his group. Although this rite became obsolete in the Rabbinic period, the third and seventh days still make terminal points in the period of mourning. The mourner is still segregated from his community and is forbidden to work and leave his house, except on Sabbath and holydays.

Other customs—some of which have legal sanction—still practiced among Jews that reveal fear and the consequent need to avoid contact with the dead are the following:

1. *Washing and Perfuming the Corpse.* This was a means of removing impurity from the body, on another level, the same as the removal of the demons and spirits inhabiting the body. Since these other-worldly creatures were supposed to have a special aversion to water, the mourner was thereby encouraging the spirit to leave. At the same time, great care was taken with the corpse not to incite it to anger. In fact, a prayer was said by the attendants of a corpse asking God to help them perform their task properly so that no evil would befall them.[47] The use of perfumes and spices served the purpose of driving away the spirits.[48]

2. *Guarding the Corpse.* So important was this service that the person guarding the body was exempt from reciting the Shema. Although the rationale given is that this service was done to prevent animals and insects from touching the body, other sources confirm that the real purpose was to prevent evil demons from harming the body, for, should this happen, the corpse might become angered and take revenge on the mourners and attendants for not protecting it properly. During the middle ages, a special prayer was recited repeatedly, an acrostic of the forty-two letter name of God. The attendants of the corpse believed that through such obsessive repetition, the corpse was protected from outside harm, and they, too, were protected from the dead person's ire. It was crucial to watch the corpse closely from death to burial (Aninut), since it was during that period when the spirits actually entered the corpse. It was therefore necessary to take great precautions.[49] While the original custom was based on law, we see that it was gradually elaborated due to fear of the dead.

3. *Closing the Apertures of the Body.* The eyes of the deceased must, by law, be closed as soon as death is confirmed. It was a common belief that the dead man's ghost left the body as soon as death occurred. It might later try to return to the body, but if the eyes were closed there would be no way for the ghost to re-enter. The same applies to closing the mouth, since it was believed that the ghost or soul departs via the mouth, with the last breath. The jaws of the deceased were to be tied up if the mouth persistently opened after death. All other bodily orifices were, by law, to be stopped up after the corpse was washed.[50]

4. *Burial Garments.* The grave vestments are known as "tachrichin," a loose garment pieced together simply without hems or knots. According to one interpretation, this symbolizes that the dead is thereby freed from the mundane cares of life.[51] But it is more likely the expression of a wish that the spirit leave the body as quickly and easily as possible; hence the makeshift garment.

5. *Opening Windows.* It is a popular, universal custom that as soon as death occurs, the windows of the house in which the person died should be opened. Like untied shrouds, the open windows would allow the spirit of the deceased a more speedy egress from the body and from the house where the mourners continue to live.[52] The law that the corpse "must be placed inside the house towards the door," affords an even greater encouragement for the soul or spirit to take leave, since he is situated at such a convenient place.[53]

When taken out of the house the corpse was sometimes lowered from the roof instead of proceeding out of the usual exit. Frazer offers the following explanation of this practice:

> *Ghosts are commonly credited with a low degree of intelligence, and it appears to be supposed that they can only find their way back to a house by the aperture through which their bodies were carried out.*[54]

6. *Proceeding to the Grave.* When it was time for the burial, the corpse was taken out feet first, "for if it had been carried head foremost, the eyes would have been towards the door and his ghost might find his way back." [55] It also became law that the corpse should be taken out before the mourner. The belief was that the spirit of the deceased, and other spirits as well, hovered about outside waiting to harm the living. If the coffin appears first, their attention will be drawn to the deceased, and they will forget about the living.[56] For a similar reason, men are supposed to be separated from women, since ghosts have a partiality for the latter.[57]

The funeral procession took the longest route to the grave in order to deceive the ghost. Having a limited intelligence, it may not remember a new, circuitous route and will therefore not be able to return to the house of the mourners. On the way to the grave, the cortege is supposed to halt several times for the purpose of shaking off spirits that may still be hovering about.[58]

Another popular custom whose purpose it was to drive away the spirits hovering about the grave was to throw earth and grass behind one's back, at the grave, and also on the coffin itself.[59] After the coffin is placed in the grave it is also customary to make circuits around it in order to ward off the spirits.[60]

7. *Returning from the Grave.* Precautionary measures were also taken on coming home from the interment. The Talmud specifies that no less than seven halts and sittings should be carried out. The procedure for doing so is described:

> (*The leader called out after the escort had sat down on the ground,*) '*Stand, dear (friends), stand up;*' (*and after they had walked for some distance he again called out,* '*Sit down, dear (friends), sit down.*' [61]

One reason given for this procedure is that it affords the escort the opportunity to comfort the mourners. Another reason is that it corresponds to the number of times "vanity of vanities" is mentioned in the Book of Ecclesiastes. In the middle ages, the custom began of reciting Psalm 91, verses 1 to 11, at each stop. The theme of this psalm is divine protection. This would be in consonance with the fear of the spirits still hovering above the entourage and ready to do harm. Moreover, it is even mentioned in the Shulchan Aruch that this is done because of "evil spirits." [62] A devious route was also to be taken on return from the grave the same as on proceeding to it, for the same reason.[63]

8. *Water and Death.* Since spirits have an aversion to contact with water, it was required that the hands be washed before entering the house after the funeral, as an effective means of getting rid of any spirits clinging to the mourners. A statement in the Shulchan Aruch reveals the true reason for this custom. While washing his hands the mourner should recite this prayer:

*Our hands have not shed this blood, neither have our
eyes seen it. . . . Forgive, O Lord, Thy people
Israel. . . . So shalt thou put away the innocent
blood from the midst of thee.*[64]

This prayer expresses the guilt feelings of the mourner, the
basic cause of the fear of ghosts and spirits. If it were not
for this sense of guilt, the defense of projection would not
be necessary. Washing the hands is thus an unconscious
symbolism to remove the threat of guilt, as water is a common symbol of expiation.

Once the mourners entered the house, they made sure
that all standing water was poured out. Although secondary explanations are given for this custom, the true reason
is to prevent the ghost's return to his former habitation.
The belief was that "spirits could not cross water and
therefore the ghost was in danger of falling into it." [65]

9. *Covering Mirrors.* The custom of covering mirrors or
turning them to the wall did not originate among the Jews,
but came to be a requirement as well as a popular custom.
The explanation given by Frazer is that "the soul, projected out of the person in the shape of his reflection in the
mirror, may be carried off by the ghost of the departed,
which is commonly supposed to linger about the house till
burial." [66]

10. *Lighting Candles.* It became a requirement to light a
candle in the room where the death took place for the entire period of Shivah. The purpose is to keep the spirits
away, since they are incapable of operating except in dark-
ness. "Nothing evil can enter where a light burns." [67]

Conclusion. The various customs and laws described center around the attention that Judaism has traditionally directed to the attitude of fear and the manner in which it has manifested itself in belief about the spirits of the dead and the harm which they can cause.

What we know today as the defense mechanisms of self-punishment and projection are given quasi-recognition in the mourning customs of Judaism. Important devices established both by law and custom are found, on examination, to be employed by the ego for its own protection against the painfulness of anxiety. The source that gives rise to these two defenses is ambivalence toward the deceased more than the frustration of love impulses which death causes. Repression is more commonly employed by the ego in relation to the latter, which gives rise to the state of anxiety.

The defenses of projection and self-punishment arise mainly after the ego has already failed to adjust to the death of a loved object. Many of the popular folk-customs connected with the bereavement situation have not been found intellectually acceptable in Jewish legal tradition because it was felt instinctively that they stem from defense mechanisms which are psychologically unwholesome. In spite of this, Judaism has recognized in actual practice that these defenses have become so extremely common because the ego is weakened under the impact of the traumatic situation which death engenders. Therefore, many of the popular customs expressing the two defenses have been accepted as requisite practices. Thus, the instinctive wisdom of Jewish law foreshadows the findings of psychoanalytic research and theory.

The customs and laws discussed above are to a degree

comparable to those developed in other civilizations throughout the world. The vast majority of them do serve the deepest needs of the mourner, even though some of them may be rationally objectionable in the more advanced civilizations. Their universality is commensurate with the universality of the feelings involved in grief. No culture can ignore these needs, for this would only create greater needs and more serious problems. The laws and customs, however primitive, do serve as an outlet for the painful feeling of the mourner.

However, Judaism as a more advanced legal system and culture, is not concerned with the mere satisfaction of these needs. The laws and customs must be sublimated from their crude, primitive form, adapted via syncretism until they become genuinely therapeutic techniques which are psychologically effective in helping the mourner to adjust to the loss and the distressful feelings that it produces, however difficult this adjustment may be.

The next chapter will examine the mourner's return to a meaningfully patterned life without the deceased, as seen in the cultural and legal framework of the mourning customs of Judaism.

1. Jones, *op. cit.*, p. 387.

2. Sem. 10:2; see Jackson, *op. cit.*, pp. 127–128.

3. II Sam. 19:1.

4. Cf. Frazer, *op. cit.*, I and II, *passim;* Hartland, *op. cit.*, p. 438.

5. Lev. 19:28; also 21:4; Deut. 14:1.

6. M. Makkot 3:5.

7. SA, YD 344:11.

8. *The Fathers according to Rabbi Nathan,* trans. Judah Goldin ("Yale Judaica Series," Vol. X, ed. Julian Obermann; New Haven: Yale University Press, 1955), No. 25, p. 110; Sem. 9:2; San. 68a.

9. Gen. R. 96.

10. Schauss, *op. cit.*, p. 272.

11. Theodor H. Gaster, *The Holy and the Profane* (New York: William Sloane Associates Publishers, 1955), p. 162; see Anderson, *op. cit.*, p. 48.

12. Joel 2:12.

13. SA, YD 396:1.

14. Morris Jastrow, Jr., "The Tearing of Garments as a Symbol of Mourning," *JAOS,* XXI (1900), 24.

15. *Ibid.*, p. 34; cf. Isaiah 32:11; Micah 1:8.

16. BK 17a; MK 22b; Sem. 9:5.

17. II Sam. 15:30; Ezek. 24:17; MK 15b; Sem. 6:1; SA, YD 380:1.

18. SA, YD 376:4.

19. SA, YD 382:1.

20. Eccl. R. 7:5; Sem. 10:5 (p. 381); SA, YD 358:3; also CHL, p. 132, note 11 ("Bet Yosef"); Gaster, *op. cit.*, p. 170.

21. Deut. 26:14. See the following for examples of fasting: I Sam. 31:13; II Sam. 1:12; 3:35; 12:16, 23; Ezra 10:6; Daniel 10:3. The law of tithed food is mentioned in M. Pes. 8:8; Sem. 12:1.

22. BB 60b; SA, YD 376:4; 402:12.

23. MK 23b; Sem. 10:4; SA, YD 341:1; for comparable examples, see Frazer, *op. cit.*, I, 198ff.

24. II Sam. 12:16; Isaiah 3:26; Jer. 14:2; Job 2:13.

25. II Sam. 1:2; Ezek. 27:30; Esther 4:3; Job 2:8; Matt. 11:21; Luke 10:13.

26. Ned. 56a; MK 14a–b, 26b; 27a; Sem. 6:1. The reason given for the change in the custom from sitting on the ground to sitting on low stools applies to most changes that have taken place in mourning customs. The Shulchan Aruch states that the change occurred because "the Gentiles will say that it is (a kind) of sorcery." SA, YD 387:1–2. As the Jews were increasingly exposed to the non-Jewish world they became more self-conscious and aware of differences from their own customs, with the result that customs offensive to non-Jews underwent gradual alteration or modification. (See concluding chapter for applications to the situation today.)

27. Sem. 6:13.

28. Francis Brown, S. R. Driver, and Charles A. Briggs, *A Hebrew and English Lexicon of the Old Testament* (Oxford: Clarendon Press, 1906), p. 871; see Psalm 38:7; Jer. 14:2; BM 59b. Another theory states that black clothing was worn as a means of identifying with the deceased. While this may be true to some extent, the emphasis is placed on self-abjection throughout the Jewish sources (see Jackson, *op. cit.*, pp. 65–66; Fenichel, *op. cit.*, p. 394).

29. Schauss, *op. cit.*, p. 287; Gaster, *op. cit.*, pp. 154–155. For comparable examples, see Frazer, *op. cit.*, I, *passim*.

30. Lev. 21:5; Deut. 14:1; Isaiah 12:12; Jer. 7:29; 16:6; Ezek. 7:18; Amos 8:10; Micah 1:16; M.Makkot 3:5.

31. Sem. 6:11; SA, YD 380:1; 390:1.

32. MK 18a; SA, YD 390:7.

33. *Clothing:* MK 15a; 23a; SA, YD 380:1; 389:1–8. *Intercourse:* MK 15b; Sem. 6:1; SA, YD 380:1; 383:1–2. *Study:* MK 15a;

Sem. 6:1; SA, YD 380:1; 384:1–5. *Bathing:* Dan. 10:2; Ta'anit 13b; MKb; Sem. 6:1; SA, YD 380:1; SA, YD 380:1.

34. Irion, *op. cit.,* p. 48.

35. Bendann, *op. cit.,* pp. 57, 81; see also Howard Becker and David K. Bruner, "Attitudes toward Death and the Dead, and some Possible Causes of Ghost-Fear," *Mental Hygiene,* XV, 834.

36. Freud, *Totem and Taboo,* p. 855. He goes on to make the following remarks: "The mourning originating from the enhanced tenderness, became on the one hand more tolerant of the latent hostility, while on the other hand it could not tolerate that the latter should not give origin to a feeling of pure gratification. Thus there came about the repression of the unconscious hostility through projection, and the formation of the ceremonial in which fear of punishment of demons finds expression (p. 856)."

37. Lev. 19:31; 20:6; Deut. 18:11; I Sam. 28.

38. Ginzberg, *op. cit.,* V, 108; Trachtenberg, *op. cit.,* p. 61; *JE,* III, 458.

39. Trachtenberg, *op. cit.,* p. 66; Ginzberg, *op. cit.,* I, 123.

40. Trachtenberg, *op. cit.,* pp. 65–66; Schauss, *op. cit.,* p. 271.

41. KSA 26:1; see also Shabbat 152b–153a.

42. Schauss, *op. cit.,* p. 271.

43. Malinowski, *op. cit.,* p. 50; Freud, *Totem and Taboo,* p. 824.

44. Lev. 21:1–2; 22:4; Nu. 5:2; 19:11, 14; Deut. 26:14. For comparable examples, see Frazer, *op. cit.,* I, 314ff; III, 175.

45. M. Middot 2:2; MK 14bff; Sem. 5:10; 6:11.

46. Nu. 19:9ff.; see Trachtenberg, *op. cit.,* p. 180.

47. Gaster, *op. cit.,* p. 164; Trachtenberg, *op. cit.,* pp. 175–176; *Hamadrikh. The Rabbi's Guide,* ed. Hyman E. Goldin (New York: Hebrew Publishing Company, 1939), XXII, 8, p. 119.

48. Gaster, *op. cit.,* pp. 164–165.

49. SA, YD 341:6; Sperka, *op. cit.,* p. 32; Trachtenberg, *op. cit.,* p. 175; Schauss, *op. cit.,* p. 291.

50. SA, YD 352:4; Schauss, *op. cit.,* p. 288; Gaster, *op. cit.,* p. 160.

51. KSA 197:1; *Hamadrikh* XXII, 7, p. 118; Gaster, *op. cit.,* p. 163.

52. *Hamadrikh* XIX, 8, p. 109; Gaster, *op. cit.*, p. 158.

53. *Hamadrikh* XXII, 16, p. 121.

54. Frazer, *op. cit.*, I, 455–456; SA, YD 353:3.

55. Schauss, *op. cit.*, p. 389; *The Book of Life*, ed. Barnett Elzas (New York: Bloch Publishing Company, 1930), p. 16.

56. KSA 197:8; Trachtenberg, *op. cit.*, pp. 177–178.

57. KSA 198:10; Trachtenberg, *op. cit.*, p. 178. (Zohar, Vayakhel, 196a–b).

58. Schauss, *op. cit.*, p. 289; Gaster, *op. cit.*, p. 172; SA, YD 358:3.

59. SA, YD 376:4; Gaster, *op. cit.*, pp. 173–175; Schauss, *op. cit.*, p. 288; Trachtenberg, *op. cit.*, p. 301, note 53.

60. Gaster, *op. cit.*, pp. 144, 163.

61. BB 100b.

62. SA, YD 376:4; Trachtenberg, *op. cit.*, p. 179; Schauss, *op. cit.*, p. 291; Gaster, *op. cit.*, p. 148.

63. Freehof, *op. cit.*, I (1944), 131.

64. SA, YD 376:4; see Gaster, *op. cit.*, pp. 174–175; Schauss, *op. cit.*, p. 268; Trachtenberg, *op. cit.*, p. 179; Freehof, *op. cit.*, I, 132.

65. SA, YD 339:5; Schauss, *op. cit.*, p. 290; Trachtenberg, *op. cit.*, pp. 176–177; Gaster, *op. cit.*, pp. 170–171.

66. CHL, p. 237, note 10; Schauss, *op. cit.*, p. 292.

67. *The Book of Life*, p. 24; Schauss, *op. cit.*, p. 268; Trachtenberg, *op. cit.*, p. 180; Gaster, *op. cit.*, p. 167; CHL, p. 241, note 22. See Shulchan Aruch, Orach Chayyim, 548, B'er Hetev, note 1.

PART THREE

The Mourning Process
in Judaism

VI

The Sociocultural
Conditions of Mourning

Introduction. Judaism, which has developed as a cultural phenomenon as well as a belief-system, emphasizes that throughout the process of mourning the bereaved must continue relating to others. This applies also when the members of the Jewish group face other common crises such as birth, marriage, and illness, as well as death.

This chapter will now answer the following questions: First, is there a therapeutic significance to the laws, standards, and ceremonies which pertain to death and mourning in the Jewish culture? Is the authority of the culture therapeutically beneficial in itself? Second, does bereavement as a communal or public activity have therapeutic significance? Third, does bereavement represent a family crisis as well as an individual and communal crisis in the Jewish tradition, and what significance does this have for the mourner's eventual recovery?

Acceptance of Cultural Authority. The prescriptions developed by the culture of the bereaved individual to meet such a crisis as the death of a loved object are commonly accepted because of the individual's own weakness and confusion. They are imprinted in the socialization process, as the culture develops the necessary provisions for facing death. The bereaved person usually accepts them since he does not know what else to do. Even when the modes of reacting to these impulses and anxieties, developed in the culture in which he lives, are not entirely in consonance with the mourner's own feelings, he tends to accept them since he has no other recourse in his time of weakness and bewilderment. If the mourning customs within the culture are too greatly in conflict with the bereaved person's own feelings and needs, then his inability to adapt to this role could be as painful as the loss itself, and the culture thus would only be intensifying conflictual feelings. When, on the other hand, the sociocultural provisions and prescriptions are in keeping with basic needs of the individual, the conflict between the bereaved person and the expectations of his society will be minimal. Some degree of conflict is, however, unavoidable.

One of the most important needs of the mourner is consistency. From the moment of birth the individual is exposed to certain value orientations and influences of his group, acquiring specific habits, roles, behavior patterns, and ways of thinking and feeling. If there is a consistent pattern within this system, the individual will be more secure, knowing what to expect and what is expected of him, whenever he must face a particular crisis, such as the death of a loved object.

As a sociocultural system, Judaism maintains a consistent attitude towards life. Whether the individual faces puberty, marriage, illness, or death, life is portrayed as a divine blessing. It is to be encountered openly, even the death of a loved object, for it is all part of the divine scheme.[1] Because of its all-encompassing nature, no individual can ignore his culture. Any conflicts that the individual may have with it will only harm the individual and not the system.

The Jewish culture is consistent in providing that among mourners no distinction should be made between rich and poor.[2] Although there was some class stratification, the critical situation which a death created required social regulation and uniformity to be imposed in the ceremonies and procedures in order to avoid inconsistency within the sociocultural system, as well as jealousies and rivalries which might be a threat to the authority of the structure, and cause the sociocultural system to lose its effectiveness in providing for the needs of the mourner.

The Jewish view is reflected in the law which requires Avelut to be cancelled for those days which fall during a festival: "A positive precept incumbent on the community overrides one incumbent on him as an individual . . . an individual's function cannot come and put off that of the public." [3] In the case of a festival's lasting eight days, the entire period of Shivah could be annulled. If the death occurs during the festival, the coffin may not be set down in a public thoroughfare because it might "give occasion for lamentation." [4]

While this law might run counter to the personal needs of the mourner, it nevertheless protects the authority and solidarity of the group. It also expresses the fundamental theme which underlies all the festivals in the Jewish culture: the goodness and blessedness of life. This emphasis on life helps to strengthen the group, in the face of the death and mourning experience, which may be socially disruptive. The annulment of Shivah or of part of Avelut through the authority of the mourner's culture helps to counter the personal hurt. The authority must be "right." It is only when the mourner doubts this that the precedence of group values may have harmful consequences to the individual.

The cultural authority of Judaism prescribes a definite role for the mourner, regardless of his own feelings. He must act like a mourner in his society, and he must be concerned with what others think of him. For example, "a mourner should not set an infant on his knee, because the child may abuse him and he may thereby incur censure from his fellow men." [5] The mourner is required to accept the proper role in order to be a part of his cultural structure.

Judaism nevertheless recognizes that the mourner may have individual needs, outside of the provisions and prescriptions of the group. A distinction is made, for example, between "Private Mourning" and "Public Mourning." On the third day after burial a mourner is allowed to work, but only in private. A woman can "work privately in her house so long as her neighbors do not see her." [6] Although the festivals may cancel part of Shivah or of Shloshim, the mourner is required to observe the rules and rites of Private Mourning. [7]

The same is required of mourners of a suicide or a victim of capital punishment. Public Mourning is not carried out for the criminal and the murderer because of the threat to the solidarity and continuity of the group implicit in their crimes against society. The suicide is equally guilty, according to Jewish law, since he has voluntarily removed himself from the group. Private Mourning, however, is permissible. Judaism recognizes that the survivors are nevertheless disturbed by their loss, "since grief is felt only in the heart." [8]

Death as a Communal Event. Judaism views death as a communal event as well as a personal crisis. The death of a member of the group affects the entire group and not only the surviving relatives. This is especially true when the group is sufficiently small for some pattern of relationship to exist among all the members. Such a group is an "affectional group" [9] since everyone is related to everyone else in some way. Even in a slightly larger group, the interrelationship among the majority of its members may be sufficiently close to view the death of any one of its members as a serious loss. In such cases, mourning rites are displayed on a communal basis, since the death of any member of the group threatens the entire group with disintegration.

A group or community, like an individual, is concerned with self-preservation when it is closely-knit and possesses an overall character, an organic identity and unity. Each member of such a group is aware, perhaps unconsciously, of its unifying force and character; hence when a member dies, the group tends to preserve itself by observance of mourning ceremonies.

This has applied, generally speaking, from Biblical times to the present day, in relatively self-contained Jewish communities. Of course, the importance of the deceased member within the community affects the group's reaction.

An intense degree of mourning was observed by the "community" upon the death of Moses.[10] In post-Biblical times, a more intense degree of mourning was expressed for rabbis and other scholars, since they were the leaders of the community,[11] and their death was a greater threat to group preservation than the death of other members.

Public rites and laws of mourning observed by the group serve the purpose of reintegrating "the group's shaken solidarity,"[12] bringing the group together again and acting as a solidifying force in the face of the serious loss caused by the death of one of its important members.

In the Jewish community, the communal aspect of every death was acknowledged as soon as any individual died. It was the custom to announce every funeral by blowing a "funerary bugle."[13] All the people in the community heard the sound and were made to feel involved in the event.

When a person died without leaving any survivors required to observe the mourning period and the rites, it became the duty of the community to appoint ten men (known as "worthy people") to sit for the first seven days after burial. It was also incumbent on the rest of the community to "assemble unto them." If it was impossible to find ten men who could sit through the entire seven days, it was permissible to organize shifts. Thus, the community was required to participate in the death of every member.[14]

The "golden rule" that every member of the community must do for others what he would expect them to do for him applied:

. . . . if one laments, others will lament for him; if one assists at burial, others will bury him; if one bears the bier, others will bear him; if one raises (his voice) others will raise (their voice) for him.[15]

It was legally required also for every person, who saw a corpse on the way to burial, to accompany the entourage. This prescription was regarded as so important that even if a student was engaged in studying the Torah, he had to suspend his studies to walk with the entourage. Those who were not engaged in Torah were forbidden to engage in their ordinary occupations from the time the person died until he was buried.[16]

It may be questioned whether any of these laws are motivated by fear of the deceased. But such laws, in Jewish culture, are based more on the fear of group disintegration than on the need to appease the ghost of the deceased. This is confirmed by the law that all mourning rites must be observed even for the apostate, who has removed himself from the Jewish community.[17] He creates the same threat to the community as the member who dies.

Death as a Family Crisis. The death of every person is especially felt within an "affectional group" in which every member is related to every other member in some way. The primary "affectional group" is the family; hence bereavement is primarily a family crisis.

The intensity of grief is in direct proportion to the libidinal attachments developed between deceased and bereaved. In the smaller community, a bereavement is a communal affair, but in a larger community it is less critical. It is, of course, most critical in the primary group—that is, the family, which is bound to be most affected by the death of one of its members.

If the deceased was the most important member of the family the living patterns of the group may become disorganized upon his death, thereby threatening the solidarity and preservation of the entire family. If the family was disorganized to some extent before the death, the death may hold them together by making them more dependent on each other.

Each member of the family group has his own individual needs and feelings, which may lead to different reactions on the part of each. One might react overtly to the loss, while another might try to suppress his feelings; one might recover more quickly than another; one may be more able to give comfort than another who needs more to receive it. These factors naturally complicate the process of mourning for each individual within the family.

When a death occurs, the roles and behavior patterns of all members in the family unit may have to be altered. These shifting roles and new adjustments tend to intensify grief. Besides, conflicts may develop among the members which may hinder the process of mourning by adding new worries and concerns to those already existing.

For example, if the father dies, the family is left without its symbol of authority. Two brothers may compete for this role, one of whom the other members may find difficult to accept as a substitute for the father. Conflicts can then intensify the grief situation. If there is nothing holding the family together, the disorganization and disintegration of the family as a unit may be accelerated.

The Talmud expresses the difficulties of bereavement involving the family in the imagery of the "Angel of Death." For the first seven days (Shivah), the angel's sword is drawn and menaces the entire family. Then, for thirty days (Shloshim), the sword swings back and forth like a pendulum. It is not put back into its sheath until the completion of the twelve months mourning period. However, if a boy was born in the family, the sword was sheathed at once.[18] The death of an individual occurred when the Angel of Death placed the sword into his mouth.[19] In Talmudic lore, the sword therefore came to represent death as much as did the Angel of Death.

How can we interpret the account just described? Fear of the deceased is based on feelings of guilt within the family group. During the mourning period, every member of the family may therefore feel threatened. Thus, the family as a group is seriously affected by the death. A male born into the family undoubtedly symbolizes the reintegration of the group; hence, it removes the angel's sword. The new member takes the place of the one who has died, thereby restoring to the family its former number and strength.

The cohesiveness of the Jewish family at the critical time of death appears in the stipulations about which relatives are required to mourn. In Biblical times, the laws of Avelut involved the wife or husband, the mother or father, the brother or single sister, and the son or daughter. Except for mourning for a married brother (probably because of the importance of the male in Biblical times), the married sister was largely excluded from these requirements since she had left the close family group through her marriage. The male usually stayed within the family unit, and his wife became part of his family, but females left their families to join their husbands' families.

In the Talmudic period, the list of those for whom one must mourn was extended to include, in addition to the above, married sisters, grandparents, grandchildren, aunts and uncles. The mourning period involved was the thirty-day period. Mourning for twelve months applied only to one's parents.[20] This extension points up the Jewish view of the family as a small community, and also emphasizes the intimate relationship between first and third generations.

Conclusion. The mourner, as part of his sociocultural system, is affected by the laws and mores developed within his community or group. These require him to assume the mourner's role defined and developed for his group, whose purpose is its own preservation and continuity. The clear definition of the mourner's role avoids chaos and prevents excessive disorganization within the community.

When the members of a community are related to each other in an "affectional" way, a death becomes a communal crisis. The family group is similarly affected by the death of one of its members.

In Judaism, the recognition of the crisis that death causes, both in the community and the family, was acutely summarized in the midrashic statement:

> *It was taught: A company and a family are like a heap of stones. You remove one stone and the whole becomes loose, while you put one stone on and the whole stands firm.*[21]

It is therapeutic for the mourner to realize that upon the death of his loved object he is not alone in his grief, for others share the profound loss with him. Even though the role as a mourner which his sociocultural system provides may conflict with his own feelings to some extent, at least he is not bewildered. He knows what is expected of him. The feeling that the culture is authoritative and therefore "right" in its prescriptions gives him a sense of confidence in what he is doing in relation to the deceased. The other members of the community and the family share his mourning with him which increases his consolation and strengthens his confidence that he is doing the right thing.

The familial and communal participation in mourning in Judaism helps and encourages the mourner to recover from the loss of his loved object. It now remains to examine the therapeutic significance of the cultural provisions which are made in Judaism relative to the mourning process.

1. The "divine scheme" is, of course, the basic foundation and ultimate *raison d'etre* of authoritativeness in the Jewish culture. Traditional Judaism maintains that all legal prescriptions and ceremonial provisions are sanctioned by God; they are therefore of a transcendent nature. The common attitude revealed in the Jewish sources is that these prescriptions and provisions must be fulfilled if the creator of the universe has ordained them. There can then be no question of their authoritative nature. The authority of the culture was further strengthened because of the guilt that the individual would feel if he transgressed those enactments sanctioned not only by the culture but by God through the covenant initiated at Mount Sinai.

2. MK 27a–27b.

3. MK 14b.

4. M. MK 3:8.

5. MK 26b; see Ecclesiasticus 38:17.

6. Sem. 6:6–7.

7. MK 24a; SA, YD 399:2; KSA 219:1.

8. Sem. 2:7; also 2:1; SA, YD 345:1. The distinction between personal need and communal provision is also reflected in the passage stating that "lamenting is internal and mourning is external (Lam. R. 7)."

9. Eliot, "Bereavement: Inevitable but not Insurmountable," p. 643.

10. Deut. 34:8.

11. MK 24a; 25a; 25b.

12. Malinowski, *op. cit.*, p. 53.

13. MK 27b; also Meg. 29a.

14. SA, YD 376:3. That the death of an individual was considered a communal crisis is also evidenced in the following law: "If the deceased is transported on a bier, the people manifest their grief; if he is not transported on a bier, it is unnecessary for them to demonstrate their grief." (SA, YD 353:5) A child under twelve months was not carried on a bier. Thus by twelve months, every member is considered a loss to the entire community.

15. MK 28b.

16. Ber. 18a; Meg. 29a; Sem. 11:7; SA, YD 343:1; 361:1; 361:3–4; *Hamadrikh* XXIII, 6–7, p. 124. A distinction was made, however, between the large community and the small community. In regard to the former it was realized that each person could not feel affected by every death. Moreover, in the large community every death was not necessarily a threat to group preservation as was the case in the small community (see Sem. 1:7; SA, YD 343:1).

17. CHL p. 98, note 24 ("Bet Lechem Yehudah").

18. SA, YD 394:4; Schauss, *op. cit.*, p. 285.

19. AZ 20b.

20. SA, YD 385:1–3.

21. Gen. R. 100:7.

VII

The Struggle for
Recovery

Introduction. Is the legal and cultural mourning system of Judaism consonant with what we now recognize as an effective therapeutic process? It incorporates a full recognition of the problems involved in grief, an outlook and valuation of the crises of life, which is consistent with the total Jewish culture, and provision for communal and familial as well as individual participation in the mourning process.

Are the methods developed in Judaism for the actual handling of the grief responses equally sound, and do they facilitate the eventual recovery of the bereaved individual?

Anxiety, which is the cause of the painfulness of the grief situation, derives from the two sources: frustration of love impulses (libidinal energy) and feelings of guilt (derived from ambivalence). While unwholesome mechanisms of defense are just as apt to crop up in the therapeutic methods developed by Judaism, as in other cultures, it will be noticed that most of these are utilized as secondary measures. Judaism attempts to develop an effective therapeutic approach by avoiding such defenses.

The Work of Mourning. Freud and Lindemann made important observations on the process, which they termed "the work of mourning" and "grief work" respectively,[1] suggesting that the average mourner undergoes stages in his reaction to his loss.

The first stage, really the first task of the mourner, is to face the reality of death, and come to acceptance of the fact that the loved one is actually dead. The traumatic shock of death is so great that the mourner may try to save himself these painful feelings either by denial or by repressing them. Through reality testing, the mourner may avoid utilizing the unsatisfactory defense of repression.

The second stage of the work of mourning involves reality testing which requires detaching one's emotional ties from the deceased, without resorting to defenses which mask or cover up the suffering that this engenders. "Man never willingly abandons a libido-position;" hence, this task involves an enormous struggle. The more the mourner tries to sever his ties with the deceased, the greater the intensification of his guilt feelings. This is one of the reasons why the mourning period usually lasts so long. Detachment is also hampered by the natural difficulty of relinquishing any dependency needs that may have existed between the bereaved and the loved object.

The third phase of grief work involves the establishment of new relationships. This phase continues throughout the period of mourning. The mourner detaches himself from the deceased by attaching himself to other persons, interests, and objects. This substitution brings about the final adjustments necessary for the recovery of the mourner, and redirects the love impulses which were originally directed to the deceased.

In all these phases, the suffering and pain involved is actually therapeutic in itself. This is the only way to come to grips with one's grief. There is no other way to approach recovery from the loss than through the pain of detaching oneself from the loved object. Substituting other persons and objects for the deceased may not be easy, but it is the only way to become part of life and of the living again.

The Realistic Attitudes of Judaism. The general attitude of Judaism to death helps the bereaved person to face the reality of death and to prevent its denial. Being resigned to the inevitable finds expression throughout the Jewish sources. The view is repeatedly expressed that birth implies death, that life itself includes death and is not totally different from it. The philosophical concept of death as the ultimate fulfillment of life, and that death is even better than birth, is expressed in these words:

> . . . . *none knows, on the day of his birth, what his deeds will be, but at his death, his good deeds are published unto all. . . .*[2]

This is similar to Rabbi Meir's interpretation of the words "tov meod." He transcribed them as "tov mot," meaning that "death is good," referring to the Biblical story of creation. At the moment when God created life, He also created death. As life itself is good, so is death, since both emanate from God.[3]

In Judaism, life is not merely a prelude to an after-life. The joy and importance of this life are consistently stressed. Nevertheless, Judaism reflects the importance of facing death. Existence is viewed in its totality which encompasses the end as well as the beginning, and the advice is given that throughout life the endeavor should be made to comprehend death. As one Hassidic rabbi stated it, "All my life has been given to me merely that I might learn to die." [4]

Every important event in life needs preparation of some kind, death not excepted. This fosters resignation to the inevitable. A person should be prepared for death. When King Hezekiah was gravely ill, the prophet Isaiah said to him: "Set thy house in order; for thou shalt die, and not live." [5]

This attitude that death is universal and unavoidable, and should therefore be confronted realistically,[6] is characteristic of the Bible. The needed preparation for death should be part of the natural order of living. It is only the fear of dying which prevents man from thinking about it and preparing for it.

The advice to think about death may appear morbid in modern times, but it was considered a necessity in Rabbinic literature. There is an account in the Talmud about Rabbi Simeon bar Halafta, who went to a circumcision ceremony. The father of the child offered the guests a wine of good quality, and then stored some away to use in later years when his son would be married. On his way home from the feast, Simeon was met by the Angel of Death, who looked disconsolate. Simeon asked the reason. The angel replied: "On account of the talk of human beings who say, 'This and that we will do,' and yet not one of them knows when he will be summoned to die." [7] Such stories were meant to instill a sense of sobriety into life. Awareness of the finality of life should not cause morbidity or fear, but should rather establish an equilibrium, the conviction that the "golden mean" is the ideal.

In Jewish literature, death is the inevitable fate of man, since it is a divine decree.[8] Instead of hoping that death will somehow end, Judaism asserts that life will continue in another form. Beliefs regarding immortality were never really systematized and elaborated in Judaism, and have always been secondary to the importance placed on life. Life is still much more to be desired than death, or any state of existence after life.

The emphasis on life in Judaism actually provides a wholesome approach to the problem of death. Through comprehension of the meaning of death, the significance of life increases. This avoids the need to shirk reality, and therefore the totality of the experience of living can be fully embraced.

It is for this reason that even at the very moment of death, the survivors are expected to confirm God's existence by reciting the "Shema" seven times. Moreover, when the garments are rent, the mourners recite: "The Lord gave and the Lord hath taken away," [9] emphasizing the importance of affirming life, while at the same time resigning oneself to death. The two values are inseparable in Judaism.

During the period immediately after death, another prayer, the "Tsidduk ha-Din," is recited. This prayer emphasizes God's attribute of justice and man's dependence on God. It asserts that what is important to God is not the length of a man's life. It also stresses that God is justified in all of his acts, including that of decreeing death.

When the grave is covered with earth, another moment of intense emotional pain, the mourner is expected to move away several feet and recite the "Kaddish." [10] Thus at the moment of severest grief, the mourner must affirm God's will and his plan. During the first meal at the house of mourning after the funeral, a special benediction is recited in the "Birkat ha-Mazon," which affirms God's justice, emphasizes that God blesses the living, and expresses the hope that the painfulness of separation will be allayed. [11]

By viewing death within the natural order of events, it becomes as natural to grieve as it is to die. Death is not disguised, so grief need not be expressed deviously or deceptively. One attitude follows from the other. The pain of separation must be confronted and expressed.

The Funeral Experience. The funeral is not only a necessary ceremony in consequence of a death, but can be extremely beneficial emotionally. For it to have a therapeutic effect, the following are the most important criteria:

> *It should avoid any artificial or unreal atmosphere. It should not deny the fact of death even though it is concerned with relating the incident of death to a larger perspective of life. It should encourage the reality sense, help people to accept the pain of loss, and avoid the tendencies toward escape that easily develop.* [12]

The one fundamental purpose of the funeral should be to encourage the mourner to face the reality of death. In accomplishing this objective, it helps the mourner to avoid repression, denial, and other defenses which would only hinder the therapeutic process of mourning.

From the time a person is actually in the process of dying, "it is an obligation to stand by him while his soul departs . . . ," [13] so that the face of the dying person can be clearly seen. Thus, by sharing with the dying person the actual moments of death, the survivors are prevented from denying their loss. Witnessing the dying person in his last moments serves as a corroboration of death. "When the body is not in evidence, it is easier to convert grief into disbelief." [14]

The view that death is a natural occurrence obviates a fear of death as a mysterious, uncanny phenomenon. Many of the ceremonies and laws in Judaism emphasize this need to realize the reality and finality of death.

The various body-centered activities required of the mourner in Judaism, such as washing and watching the corpse, further encourage the sense of reality. There is a discussion in the Talmud over whether spices and perfumes can be brought into a house of mourning. A distinction is made between a "house of mourning" and a "house of comforters." The former term is used when the corpse is still in the house, and the latter when the corpse is no longer present. The conclusion is that spices and perfumes may not be brought into a house of mourning while the corpse is still there, but are permissible in a house of comforters. One possible reason for this ruling is that the smell of the corpse would serve to heighten the sense of reality, and help to prepare the mourners for the departure of the body. It would make them realize that the loved one is really dead.[15]

The funeral eulogy is also intended to stress the finality and the loss. Several passages in the Talmud, taken from funeral eulogies, emphasize the termination of life and the severe loss, rather than glossing over the death.[16]

The mourners are also required to witness the coffin being lowered into the grave. This stresses the sense of reality. As soon as the deceased is covered with earth the period of Avelut begins. This actually visualizes the separation from the deceased, making death complete and final.[17]

The coffin is made of plain wood and kept in the house of mourning until the funeral. All the laws and ceremonies emphasize that the deceased is definitely separated from the survivors. This is the fundamental purpose of Aninut: to enable the bereaved person to test reality and avoid resorting to unwholesome defenses like denial. While this struggle may be painful, it is therapeutically sound and helps bring about ultimate recovery.

Even after burial reality testing continues, during Avelut. The abstentions that the mourner must undergo help to define his relationship to the deceased, and bring the realization that the loved object is dead. Extreme forms of abstention may serve the defense of self-punishment. If a mourner is present in a House of Study, the other students must discuss the laws of mourning both at the beginning and at the end of their sessions. The mourner is never allowed to forget his role or his loss.[18]

Another law states that a woman who gave birth while in the period of the Shloshim may wear her Sabbath clothes when she goes to Synagogue, but may not wear her best clothes "lest her mind be diverted and she forget that she is in mourning." [19]

Expressing Grief. Through various laws, the mourner is required to remind himself of the death of his loved object, not only for the purpose of facing reality but also to help in giving vent to his feelings. Mourning is basically an affective process which operates to relieve the tension of frustrated love impulses. But it does so only if the mourner is capable of expressing the related emotions. As Lindemann points out, one of the most serious obstacles to accomplishing the work of mourning is that "patients try to avoid the intense distress connected with the grief experience and to avoid the expression of emotion necessary for it." [20]

When an emotion is denied expression, it is not destroyed but only pushed down into the unconscious. The pressure builds up and may manifest itself in some disguised, unwholesome form. By giving vent to the affective tension caused by the frustration of his love impulses, the mourner moves on his way toward severing his emotional ties to the deceased. The dynamic energy itself, which had been consumed in the love relationship, seeks satisfaction. Through the expression of grief this energy is used, thus bringing emotional relief to the mourner and gradually allaying the affective force of the love relationship. The mourner thereby becomes capable of detaching himself from the deceased.

The expression of grief feelings helps the mourner to achieve the second phase of the work of mourning. The mourner is repeatedly encouraged to give vent to his feelings and emotional disturbances. For example, it is expected that children, too, will rend their garments on the occasion of a death "in order to stir up sadness." [21] It is considered improper for one who is required to rend his garments to do so before he comes into the presence of the immediate relatives, for when he engages in keria in their presence, it encourages them to express their grief.[22]

Another significant law states: "Those who come (home) within three (days) should count with you; those that do not come (home) within three (days) should count by themselves." [23] This conveys the idea that during the first three days after a death, there is ample time to express one's feelings of grief along with the rest of the family. But after three days have elapsed, the mourner needs more time to express his feelings, and should therefore be allowed to count the full period of mourning for himself in order to do so.

The mourner is further encouraged to grieve by reading certain permitted literary selections. He is not allowed to read any other works except "Job, Lamentations, the sad parts of Jeremiah and the Laws of Mourning." [24]

One of the most effective ways of expressing grief is by talking to others about the deceased, his life, and the mourner's relationship to him. Talking about these memories helps the mourner to free himself of the emotional tensions that may be involved. Through oral expression, they come to the surface and are no longer hidden from consciousness. The mourner is then more capable of coming to grips with them.

In expressing his grief to other people, the mourner not only frees himself of pent-up emotional tensions connected with the deceased but also learns to form new relationships with people. Talking involves all three phases of successful mourning.[25] Listening, too, serves a therapeutic purpose. Feelings of guilt may be allayed when the mourner feels that an understanding person is listening and accepts his painful feelings, which are unacceptable to himself. The mourner has had aggressive impulses and feelings of hostility against the deceased, for which he is punished by his superego. But if others listen to him with a sympathetic and accepting attitude, his own attitudes and feelings cannot be as "wicked" as he had thought.

In Jewish law, in the presence of the corpse all topics of discussion are forbidden except "those matters which concern the dead person." During the period of Aninut, the bereaved is not to think or talk about anything else. During the period of Avelut, all who come to visit the mourner are forbidden to say anything until the mourner speaks first. In this way, the mourner is encouraged to talk about his own problems and his own grief.[26] From the beginning of his adjustment to the loss, the bereaved centers his attention on the deceased.

Crying is another effective way of expressing feelings of grief, as it is with any emotional or physical pain. Tears may unconsciously wash away or dissolve the cause of pain.

> *Whenever stimuli of grief, disappointment, anger, or "over-whelming" joy exceed the tolerance of the organism, the ensuing state of tension is alleviated by a release of energy from various organs or organ systems which abolishes the tension.*[27]

Weeping is the direct result of the state of anxiety, which arises when an overwhelming flood of stimuli seeking release is stopped up and frustrated from achieving satisfaction. Weeping serves to alleviate the emotional tension.

In the Jewish culture, as in other cultures, lamenting and weeping were first a form of appeasement resulting from fear of the dead. Yet today, they still serve the therapeutic purpose of releasing emotional tension. Weeping was encouraged in Judaism as a natural response and as a therapeutic measure.

During the Biblical period weeping was considered synonymous with mourning.[28] In post-Biblical times weeping was also encouraged. Throughout Jewish history it has been viewed as a social responsibility to weep when a member of the community has died. In the Mishna, reference is made to "a field of mourners" which was used to bewail the dead. It was situated close to the tombs of the deceased.[29]

The eulogy was employed, in part, to encourage the mourners to cry. Actually, the Hebrew word for eulogy means lamenting or wailing. Funeral oratory was a special profession. The orator's principal task was "to break the heart." He was expected to exaggerate a bit in his praise of the deceased, as well as to be fervid in his delivery, in order to encourage crying.[30] We can see, for example, in this introduction to a funeral oration, how the orator attempted to bring tears to his listeners' eyes:

Ye Palms, sway your heads (and deplore)
A Saint, a noble Palm that is no more

Who days and nights in meditation spent;
For him, day and night, let us lament.[31]

Besides professional orators, professional mourners or "wailers" were also employed. Women were especially valued for this task because of their ability to create a mood conducive to the expression of sorrow. Although there were such professional wailing women during Biblical times, it was not until Talmudic times that the profession developed its own liturgical selections, which were used repeatedly. Some of these are mentioned in the Talmud:

Cry woe o'er him that is departing!
Cry woe o'er his wounds and smarting!
Be muffled, ye high mountains,
(Clouds) covering your head;
Of high lineage and grand ancestry
Came he that is dead.
This death or that death (is the end of the quest);
Our bruises are the rate of interest.[32]

In these the emphasis is on the sorrow of death and the pain of bereavement. The mourner is encouraged not to feel inhibited in crying, to express his suffering, and to feel that his suffering is justified.

Public weeping emphasizes that mourning was considered a social responsibility. Having others join in crying helped the individual mourner to exteriorize his grief and thus to express his innermost feelings. This lack of inhibition helped to ward off denial of death and repression, bringing the related feelings into the open. The mourner was thus gradually enabled to sever his emotional ties to the deceased. Since weeping was considered a social affair, the mourner could share his grief with others and begin to establish new relationships. Thus outward expression is therapeutically efficacious in counteracting anxiety, resolving deep emotional conflicts, and helping the mourner to mend the broken fragments of his life.

Rites and Rules. The observance of the many rituals, ceremonies, and laws which Judaism has provided for the mourning period is in complete consonance with the basic psychological roots of grief. They help the mourner to counter his frustrated love impulses and his painful sense of guilt. They also aid the mourner in avoiding repression, denial, and other unwholesome defenses.

The mourning rituals and the laws which give sanction to their observance represent symbolically the deepest feelings of the mourner. They help the mourner to express unconscious feelings and control them. Giving them order and meaning leads to eventual recovery from the suffering caused by death.

> . . . *the process of symbolization is carried out unconsciously and the individual is quite unaware of the meaning of the symbol he has employed; indeed, is often unaware of the fact that he has employed one at all, or else has only been present for a time and then forgotten.*[33]

While each individual may have his own private symbols, the society or community into which he is born already possesses its own symbol-system, which represents its collective feelings, attitudes, and ideas. He is thus enabled to relate to his sociocultural system. The symbols become a part of each member of the society and enable him to become one with the cultural environment which they portray. Without them the individual would feel weak and powerless in confronting the larger environment and the world. With them the environment and the world become knowable and therefore controllable.

> *They become part of his self and his relationship with those around him, being fitted inwardly into the structure of the personality and outwardly into his relations with his species, his society, and the physical world.*[34]

Judaism provides symbols to help the individual detach himself from the deceased and become a part of his world again. Because he is overwhelmed by the traumatic situation of death, he needs established patterns in order to control his chaotic feelings, which grow out of the universal needs of the human psyche.

> *From time immemorial, religious ceremonials have offered a needed expression for mourning, and so have played an indispensable part in healing. . . . it is rare indeed not to crave the healing power of some ceremonial which joins us to others and in which we play our part.*[35]

In Judaism this need to express grief through symbolism is recognized not only implicitly but also explicitly. The Midrash reports that when Jerusalem was destroyed God went into mourning. He inquired of the angels how a human king fulfills the ceremonies of mourning. When they instructed him, he replied that he would carry out the same laws.[36] The implication is that the rules and rites are of universal significance, all-encompassing, an indigenous part of the culture; even more, culture itself. Their efficacy cannot be doubted since they express the basic needs of man.

Unlike all other laws in Judaism, mourning rituals and laws were not developed as a means of religious discipline, but rather to serve the needs of the bereaved and give structured expression to his deepest feelings. They should therefore not be onerous. There is a legal principle pertaining to mourning that the law always "follows the authority of the more lenient view." [37]

Another method adopted by Judaism, which is characteristic of religious experience in general, is the repetition of rituals. Repeating the acts helps reduce painful tensions and gives the individual the feeling that he is in control of his environment, since they represent symbolically the difficulties that he encounters in his environment. A one-time performance of a symbolic act may not be sufficient to achieve the purpose of the act.

Most of the repetitious acts in the Jewish system are performed at the beginning of the mourning period, when the bereaved person is most overwhelmed by grief. As soon as the death occurs the mourner is expected to repeat three times each of the following two liturgical verses: "The Lord reigneth; the Lord hath reigned; the Lord shall reign forever and ever" and "Blessed be his name whose glorious kingdom is forever and ever." Then he recites the following two verses seven times each: "The Lord he is God" and "Hear O Israel, the Lord our God, the Lord is one." [38]

While the corpse is being prepared for burial, the person who washes it repeats verses from the Bible concerning cleanliness and concludes by repeating three times the

"Taharah" (Purification).[39] When the deceased is put into the grave, the bier is turned over three times.[40] Another ruling, which was practiced until the Middle Ages, concerns overturning the bed in the mourner's house.

> *The bed must be overturned six, five, four, or three times. What is the procedure? If the death occurred near sunset, then six times; if near sunset on the eve of the Sabbath, then five times; if a festival takes place the day after the Sabbath, then four times; in the case of the two days of Rosh Hashanah, then three times.*[41]

Most of the rituals throughout Avelut are repeated from day to day. The most important of these is the Kaddish which is recited by the mourner daily for eleven months. These repetitious acts slowly decrease as the mourner goes through the period of Avelut, corresponding to the gradual reduction of the mourner's need to perform them as he slowly adjusts to the loss, detaches himself from the deceased, and learns to relate to others. Judaism allows the mourner slowly to regain a sense of independence.

Conclusion. Judaism attempts to provide the mourner with various modes for the wholesome expression of grief. Through them he gains the ability to control his chaotic feelings and channel them by orderly acts and rituals. He can thus avoid resorting to pathological defenses which would only hinder his recovery. Judaism encourages talking and weeping so that the mourner may relieve the tension of his frustrated love and alleviate the pain of guilt. Through public weeping he is confirming and displaying his love for the deceased. The many symbolic acts that

Judaism has developed also serve this two-fold purpose.

Above all, the outward expressions of grief and the general attitudes toward death provided by the culture enable the mourner to face the reality of his bereavement. Since the daily acts of the mourning period keep death always before him, it is impossible for him to deny the loss of his loved object; neither can he repress thoughts or feelings associated with the deceased. Since these symbolic acts are mainly performed in the presence of others, they afford the mourner the opportunity of relating to them and detaching himself from the deceased.

The three phases of successful mourning—acceptance, detachment, and relationship—are ideally achieved through the means provided by Judaism, whose attitudes and ceremonials are emotionally beneficial.

1. Freud, "Mourning and Melancholia," *passim;* Lindemann, *op. cit.*, p. 143; see also Irion, *op. cit.*, pp. 29–30.

2. Ex. R. 48:1.

3. Gen. R. 9:5.

4. *A Treasury of Comfort,* ed. Sidney Greenberg (New York: Crown Publishers, Inc., 1954), p. 73.

5. II Kings 20:1.

6. See such passages as II Sam. 14:14; Psalms 49:1–13; Eccl. 2:14; 3:19–20.

7. Deut. R. 9:1.

8. AZ 5a.

9. *Hammadrikh* XIX, 6–10, pp. 109–111.

10. SA, YD 376:4.

11. Ber. 46b; SA, YD 379:1.

12. Jackson, *op. cit.*, p. 222.

13. SA, YD 339:4; *The Book of Life,* p. 17.

14. Eliot, "Of the Shadows of Death," p. 94; see Jackson, *op. cit.*, p. 150; Rogers, *op. cit.*, pp. 26–27.

15. MK 27a.

16. Meg. 28b; MK 25b; Sem. 8:20; Gen. R. 91:9; Eccl. R. 5:3–5; 12.

17. Sem. 1:5; KSA 199:9.

18. Sem. 10:13; also MK 23a.

19. KSA 211:11.

20. Lindemann, *op. cit.*, p. 143; see Shand, *op. cit.*, pp. 342–343; Helene Deutsch, "Absence of Grief," *PQ,* VI (1937), 21; Fenichel, *op. cit.*, p. 143.

21. MK 26b; also MK 14b.

22. MK 26b.

23. MK 22a. There are several opinions about the number of days to be counted when one returns to the house of mourning from another place. But the underlying opinion of the Talmudic debate is that a mourner should count with other mourners if he returns during the first three days. Thereafter he should participate in the remaining days of Shivah with the mourners and then count the number of days he originally missed by himself in private mourning, until he has completed seven days.

24. SA, YD 384:4; see Schauss, *op. cit.*, pp. 268–269.

25. Ina May Creer, "Grief Must be Faced," *The Christian Century* (February 28, 1945), pp. 269–270; Waller and Hill, *op. cit.*, p. 481; Rogers, *op. cit.*, p. 27; Irion, *op. cit.*, p. 27.

26. Ber. 3b; MK 28b; SA, YD 344:16; 376:1.

27. Gert Heilbrunn, "On Weeping," *PQ*, XXIV, No. 2 (1955), 245; Endre Peto, "Weeping and Laughing," *IJP*, XXVII (1946), p. 131.

28. Isaiah 16:7; Jer. 16:5; Job 30:31; see also Gen. 23:2; II Sam. 1:12.

29. M. Oholot 18:4.

30. Ber. 6b; 62a; Shabbat 153a; MK 8a; SA, YD 344:1.

31. MK 25b.

32. MK 28b; for further references to professional wailers, see the following: Jer. 9:16–17; 22:18; M. MK 3:9; M. Ket. 4:4; Meg. MK 27b; Sem. 14:7; SA, YD 344:3.

33. Jones, *op. cit.*, p. 97.

34. Lloyd W. Warner, *The Living and the Dead* ("Yankee City Series," Vol. V; New Haven: Yale University Press, 1959), p. 494.

35. Anna W. M. Wolf, *Helping Your Child to Understand Death* (New York: The Child Study Association of America, Inc., 1958), p. 61; see Malinowski, *op. cit.*, p. 52; Jackson, *op. cit.*, pp. 128–129.

36. Lam. 1:1.

37. MK 17b–18a; see MK 20a; also, Erub. 46a. For examples of the principle of leniency, see the following MK 17b; 26b; SA, YD 380:5–17.

38. *The Book of Life,* p. 17.

39. *Ibid.,* p. 22.

40. KSA 199:8.

41. Sem. 11:18.

VIII

Final Adjustments

Introduction. We have observed Judaism's insistence on facing death realistically. This is done not only through laws and ceremonies but through certain fundamental attitudes towards death. Once the bereaved accepts the loss of the loved object as permanent, it is easier for him to adjust to the new situation. Realistic confrontation with death eases the struggle to detach oneself from the deceased and from the dependency needs of the relationship, as well as from the strong emotional ties which prevail. This struggle involves two factors: frustration of love and pain of guilt feelings.

The laws, ceremonies, rituals, and observances of Judaism help the bereaved to relate to others and to feel himself a part of his community, achieving acceptance of reality and detachment from the deceased by these relationships. In this way, also, guilt is assuaged because the bereaved person learns that he is accepted by others. If others do not punish and reject him, he may come to sense that his feelings of guilt are actually unwarranted. Judaism recognizes that it takes time to alleviate the distress of bereavement.

The Group's Obligation to the Mourner. The bereaved person, for a brief period after the death of his loved object, is extremely concerned with himself. Frustration of dependency needs and the impulses of love as well as painful feelings of guilt toward the deceased makes the bereaved incapable of relating to others meaningfully. Hence the great need on the part of the community to help the mourner to become part of life once again.

The mourner is encouraged, by the attention of the community to his grief, to restore and develop meaningful relationships with those around him. If others did not care about him, and did not accept him and his suffering, the incentive to recover from grief would be destroyed.

Concern for the mourner and his needs has great therapeutic importance. Judaism gives full attention to restoring the mourner to the life of his community.

The entire funeral experience is structured as much around the mourners as it is around the deceased. The eulogy, in praising the deceased, allows the mourner to "bask in a sort of vicarious glory" [1] by identification since he has so intimately related in life to the deceased.

In the Talmud, however, some disagreement is expressed as to whether the eulogy is supposed to honor the dead or the living, or both.[2] One of the essential elements of a traditional eulogy is praise of the deceased, which in turn reflects on the mourners.[3] It accords the mourner recognition of his suffering, as can be seen in the following selection from a eulogy:

Weep you for the mourners
Not for what is lost;
He found him rest;
'Tis we are left distressed.[4]

Judaism does not ask the mourner to forget himself, but, on the contrary, his right to suffer because of his own personal loss is affirmed, and he is encouraged to mourn. The self is all-important, and the suffering it undergoes is all-important.

This emphasis is given further recognition when, after the funeral, the people assembled for the burial arrange themselves in two "Rows," through which the mourners pass receiving condolences. This custom expresses formally the consolation of the community at the mourner's loss and enables him to reveal his personal suffering in a sheltered situation amidst sympathetic relatives and friends.[5]

Self-concern and public sympathy are further encouraged at the Mourner's Meal where "the mourner reclines in the foremost place."[6] This meal serves several purposes. It satisfies the mourner's need for attention and gives acceptance to his feelings of ambivalence, allowing him to feel both unique in his sorrow and part of the group. The loss of his loved object and the frustration of his love impulses makes the mourner feel neglected and lonely. Others now give him some of the attention and personal gratification that he received from the deceased. Sitting in the foremost place at the Mourner's Meal therefore has a special significance.

The same is true of the custom prevailing in the House of Mourning. The people who visit are expected to sit still, and "as soon as the mourner nods his head the comforters are no longer allowed to remain seated by him." [7] This law affords the mourner the satisfaction of being the all-important center of attention, the object of love and compassion.

This need is exemplified in the story of several rabbis who tried to comfort Yochanan ben Zakkai after the death of his son. Each one reminded Yochanan of some other person who had experienced and overcome grief. Yochanan resented this because they did not focus their attention completely on him. But when Rabbi Eliezer, who came to comfort him, eventually concentrated all of his attention and compassion on Yochanan, he was comforted. [8]

The law states that after the first three days of Avelut a mourner may go to another house of mourning, but cannot "take a place among the comforters but among those who are (to be) comforted." [9] This recognizes the mourner's need for attention and also the difficulty of giving of himself to others during this crucial period when his need is to receive love in compensation for the love he has lost. These observances are in consonance with the psychological principle that "sorrow tends to be diminished by the knowledge that another sorrows with us." [10] The presence and sympathetic attention of others acts as a support to the bereaved, and ultimately restores him to the group. Feeling accepted and loved by others, he gradually recovers from his frustrated need to love and be loved by the deceased. Thus, others gradually take the place of the deceased, and the bereaved slowly detaches himself from the deceased and from his self-absorption.

An important part of the process of working through grief is that of withdrawing the emotional capital invested in the deceased and reinvesting it in the relationships that can continue to produce fruit in life.[11]

Psychologically, the mourner gradually transfers his libidinal energy from the deceased to persons, objects, and activities of his group, and his feelings of frustration and guilt become mollified.

This process is really one of transference or substitution. It is expressed in the Jewish culture partly through the organization known as the "Chevra Kadishah" (Holy Society), consisting of respected members of the community who volunteer for this sacred task. The duties of the Chevra Kadishah were to stay with the mourner during the night following the death, to help with all of the funeral and burial arrangements, and to organize the Mourner's Meal and the prayer services in the House of Mourning during the Shivah.[12] The Chevra Kadishah, sharing the grief with the mourner, giving him the attention and consolation he needed, as well as a sense of community, helped him to return to the group. In large communities, when it was impossible for every member to participate with every mourner, the communal responsibilities were handled by the Chevra Kadishah.

"Nichum Avelim" (comforting the mourners) was regarded as an important task of the Jewish community, and a "mitzvah" of paramount significance. As others share his grief with him, the mourner learns once again to share with others and re-establishes a continuing relationship.

The necessity of "Nichum Avelim" is stressed in such accounts as the following:

> *When the Temple was destroyed, the sages instituted (the rule) that the bridegrooms and mourners should go to the synagogues and to the houses of study. The men of the place see the bridegroom and rejoice with him; and they see the mourner and sit with him upon the earth, so that all the Israelites may discharge their duty in the service of loving kindness.*[13]

Even though a festival cancels mourning, extending comfort to mourners is still required.[14] Whereas the death of an individual is a threat to the group structure and existence, the festival celebration affirms the solidarity and preservation of the group. Hence, Nichum Avelim, which is really an expression of group solidarity, is not discontinued for a festival. Its therapeutic purpose of bringing the mourner back to the group is regarded as essential.

The Talmud states that if a mourner joins the rest of his family once they have begun Avelut, he may continue to count with his family, if he arrived within the first three days. But if he arrived after three days, he must count on his own from the time he heard the news.[15] There is another opinion, that of Rabbi Simeon, that even "if he came home on the seventh day from a place in the vicinity he counts with them." Judah ha-Nasi states that Simeon's opinion is followed only when the person returns home and finds "comforters still present." [16] In this way, the belated mourner still has the advantage of relationship with others, which gives him comfort in his grief.

In Judaism, the funeral experience, the services of the

Chevra Kadishah, and the practice of "Nichum Avelim," all encourage the mourner to re-establish meaningful relationships with others and participate in the life of the community, thereby resuming a wholesome pattern of living.

The Mourner's Obligation to the Group. When the mourner begins to feel a sense of responsibility to others, his adjustment to his loss is really underway. He has come to feel accepted by the group because of its endeavors to give him help and comfort. Thus he gradually perceives once again the significance and worth of others than the deceased and himself. There is, then, a slow transference of his love and interests from the deceased to the group, and he begins to direct his impulses and feelings of responsibility to the group. It is now no longer sufficient for the mourner to sit back and receive all the attention; he must begin to give back to the group.

This takes some time to develop. The ties to the deceased are not easily severed. Judaism does not attempt to accelerate the process.

The law, interestingly, stipulates when the greeting "Shalom" can be received and given. For the first three days of Avelut the mourner may not extend a greeting to others nor respond to one except to identify himself as a mourner. From the fourth to the seventh day, no greeting is extended but the mourner may respond if one is given to him. Then from the eighth to the thirtieth day, the mourner may both extend and respond to a greeting.[17]

These three categories structure the entire therapeutic process in Judaism. For the first few days the mourner cannot readily give to others; but he has a profound need to receive. For the next few days he learns gradually to relate to others, but still in a passive, receptive way. After Shivah is completed and for the duration of Avelut, the mourner tries to give as well as to receive, to experience reciprocity and relatedness.

As a therapeutic measure, the individual mourner is expected to face certain responsibilities to the group. For example, if there are not enough people to carry a coffin or to attend a burial, a mourner of even one day is expected to leave his house to perform these duties, although it is still optional to a degree. Moreover, a mourner is forbidden to study, but if he is needed for the purpose of giving instruction he may do so. The same applies to leading congregational prayers. The following principle applies to the mourner's responsibilities:

> . . . (*in the case of*) *every matter connected with religious duty that cannot be performed without the mourner, he is permitted to go out in order to perform the religious duty.*[18]

This principle appears in the Shulchan Aruch, but a similar principle was already established in the Talmud. After listing several things from which the mourner must abstain, the Talmud continues: "If, however, the public have need of him, he need not abstain." [19]

The mourner is thus given a definite role by the group, facing those responsibilities which "cannot be performed without the mourner." This requirement is therapeutically sound since upon the death of his loved object the mourner may feel that he is no longer wanted and serves no useful purpose. His culture renews his sense of purpose by communicating to him that he is a necessary and vital part of the group. Group acceptance and need for the mourner helps to restore him to a wholesome pattern of living.

The Therapy of Time. The work of mourning—the process of facing reality, detaching oneself from the deceased, and relating to others—is an arduous task which requires time. The depth of the relationship and the degree of intimacy and dependency, as well as the length of time during which their relationship developed, makes it impossible to accelerate the process of recovery.

Time is therefore a therapeutic factor in itself for the work of mourning, which involves a working through of complex feelings within the bereaved individual. The division of the mourning process into specific periods gives a sense of regularity and security to the mourner. Regulated sequences are marked by specific duties, clearly elucidated rites, and certain cultural expectations. The time it takes to work through grief is not a meaningless continuum, but a wisely structured sequence. This helps the mourner to feel that he has some control over the bereavement situation, and will be able to readjust to life without the deceased.

It is also therapeutically significant that there is a definite termination of mourning. The mourner knows not only what is expected of him during the period of Avelut but also that these expectations will end within a specified period. The mourner, therefore, need not feel confused or guilty about whether he has done enough. This is similar to the significance of termination in psychotherapy, when both doctor and patient understand that the time of each session is limited.

If these limitations are seen in the proper light, it will be recognized that they have real therapeutic value. The person who knows what he may do and not do, what is expected of him, what he must accept in order to achieve a certain goal, is thereby helped. The real world in which all of us live is composed of definite limitations which the mature person learns to accept without conflict.[20]

The division of the mourning year into specific periods, which give order to the mourner's life, did not occur accidentally. Its therapeutic value is stated explicitly in the following passage:

. . . in the ordinary course of things the grief of mourning goes on diminishing for seven days. It is strongest on the first day, and grows weaker and weaker till after twelve months (it disappears).[21]

This principle of gradually tapering off the severity of grief in the course of time is extended to many specific enactments. A mourner is required, for example, to remain in his house during the period of Shivah. In the second week it is permissible for him to leave his house, but he must sit in a different seat in the Synagogue for that week. In the third week he can sit in his usual place, but he is not allowed to speak. Then, in the following week, "he is like any other person." This law is extended to a period of twelve months when the deceased is a parent.[22] There are many other enactments which regulate the rituals and ceremonies of mourning in accordance with the time divisions of the mourning period.[23]

The moment when one division commences and another ends is also specified. The period of Shivah begins when the grave is covered. As soon as the sun rises, the restrictions of the seventh or the thirtieth day are completed.[24] The law that an individual in mourning for a parent is expected to cut his hair when he receives rebuke from others is not left in an ambiguous state. A mourner was expected to be rebuked at the end of three months.[25]

The end of Avelut is also marked by specific observances so that the mourner may be made completely aware of the termination of the mourning requirements. On every anniversary of the death of one's parent, the mourner is expected to recite the Mourner's Kaddish in the Synagogue. It is a religious duty to fast on that day.[26]

After the end of Avelut, no more is demanded of the mourner. He can feel confident that the deceased would be satisfied, and is consoled that he has achieved the termination of the arduous work of mourning. That the community, too, is expected to recognize the specific termination of Avelut is brought out in the following account:

> *If one meets another mourner after twelve months and tenders him (the words of) consolation, to what can he be likened? To (the case of) a man who had his leg broken and healed when a physician met him and said to him, Come to me and let me break it and set it (again), to convince you that my medicaments are good.*[27]

Conclusion. The most difficult struggle for the mourner is to sever his ties with the deceased, facing the fact that the deceased is really dead. It is achieved through the establishment of new relations, new interests, and the renewal of activity within the community to which the bereaved person belongs. By substituting other objects and persons for the deceased, the mourner becomes capable of rechannelling his libidinal energy. Feeling accepted and wanted by the community assuages his sense of guilt.

Judaism, however, recognizes that the difficult work of mourning takes time; there is no short-cut on the road to recovery. Time is, therefore, aided as a therapeutic measure, by laying down specific periods and requirements so that the mourner, who feels helpless and overcome by the agony of grief, may know exactly what is expected of him as he makes his way through the difficult period of mourning. Life thus gradually becomes more meaningful to him. His sociocultural system, being authoritative and therefore "correct," his observance of its laws and rites, makes him feel that he has also been correct and proper in his mourning.

Thus, Judaism helps the mourner to confront the emotional complexities involved in his loss, to adjust to a new life without the loved object, and to realize that there is indeed "a time to mourn."

1. Waller and Hill, *op. cit.*, pp. 554–555; see Albert A. Goldman, "Counseling the Bereaved," *CCAR Journal* (June, 1953) p. 40.

2. Sanhedrin 46b.

3. *Ibid.;* Sem. 3:6; SA, YD 344:1.

4. MK 25b.

5. Schauss, *op. cit.*, p. 267; M. Ber. 3:2; Ber. 19a; Nu. R. 10:11.

6. MK 28b; also Ket. 69b; SA, YD 376:1.

7. MK 27b.

8. *The Fathers according to Rabbi Nathan, op. cit.*, pp. 76–77.

9. MK 21b; SA, YD 393:1.

10. Shand, *op. cit.*, p. 341; see Eliot, "Bereavement: Inevitable but not Insurmountable," p. 656.

11. Edgar N. Jackson, "Grief and Religion," *The Meaning of Death*, p. 225; Eliot, "Bereavement: Inevitable but not Insurmountable," pp. 663–664.

12. "Burial Society," *JE*, III, 437; see Schauss, *op. cit.*, p. 256.

13. "Pirke de Rabbi Eliezer," p. 123.

14. SA, YD 399:1.

15. *Supra*, p. 115.

16. MK 22a; SA, YD 375:8; see also MK 28b.

17. MK 21b; SA, YD 385:1.

18. SA, YD 384:1, 3; 393:1, 3.

19. MK 21a.

20. Carroll A. Wise, *Pastoral Counseling. Its Theory and Practice* (New York: Harper & Brothers, 1951), p. 61.

21. Esther R. 8:1–2; see also Gen. R. 64:5.

22. MK 23a; Sem. 10:11; SA, YD 393:2.

23. For example, see the following SA, YD 344:10; 375:2; 394:1.

24. San. 47b; SA, YD 375:1–2; 376:4; 395:1.

25. SA, YD 390:3.

26. SA, YD 376:4.

27. MK 21b; see Sem. 14:2.

Afterword:
The Situation Today

The last two centuries or so have witnessed a considerable change in the Jewish communal structure. There has
been a widespread dissolution of the close-knit group life
which held the Jews together and enabled them to continue
observance of their indigenous laws and customs.

From Talmudic times to the eighteenth century the majority of Jews, although scattered throughout the world,
lived within a communal structure very much of their own.
The life of the average Jew was almost completely regulated by the legal system of Judaism; hence the body of
laws and customs regarding bereavement could remain
relatively unchanged, and the sociocultural system could
provide all the basic therapeutic measures needed for reso-
lution of the problems arising from the stress of grief.

But in the western societies of modern times, most Jews

have become a part of their general environments. As a result, the cultural authority of their Jewish community life has been threatened. With the beginnings of Emancipation in the West, the Jew saw his own institutions, which had remained essentially unchanged since the Talmudic period, set off against the background of the dominant culture, which stresses an entirely different set of values. Because of this phenomenon, he could no longer feel as confident and secure in the sociocultural system of Judaism as he had been down through the ages. One of the areas most affected by this shift lies in the customs and ceremonies related to the needs of the bereaved person.

In the United States especially, the majority of Jews are participants in a non-Jewish middle-class society. This trend towards assimilation can lead to the dissolution of Jewish life in the process of acculturation to the basic values and behavioral modes of the non-Jewish environment. When the American way of life becomes more influential religiously than the Jewish way of life, and the Bible and the Shulchan Aruch no longer command the authority which they once possessed in the Jewish community, there is a danger that many precious assets hallowed over the centuries and proven in use, may be lost.

We have seen that the average Jew's attitudes towards death and his mourning observances show a remarkable consonance with sound psychiatric knowledge and with the best that we know about the therapy of grief. Any drastic alteration in the patterns of grief expression among Jews which would lead them away from the sociocultural system of mourning in Judaism, described and documented in this book, and towards conformity with the general patterns of handling death, bereavement and mourning in contemporary American society would be a serious regression.

Great differences exist between the two cultures in both values and attitudes, and in individual and communal rites and customs. In our modern American society, death is made to seem a remote phenomenon. Sickness has become more preventable and curable, and the life-span has been increased phenomenally. Most people die in the antiseptic atmosphere of large hospitals where death seems almost to be impersonal, rather than at home surrounded by grieving loved ones, as they usually did in the past. Hence, when death is not actually denied, as indeed it cannot well be, it is de-emphasized. In this situation death tends to lose its meaning as a fact of life.

The conquest of diseases and the lengthening of the life-span do not in any wise affect the inevitability and universality of death. Any way of life which fails to accord full recognition to this fact fosters unwholesome mental mechanisms like denial and repression, and does its adherents no service.

Along with this denial or de-emphasis of death, in the contemporaneous American culture the bereaved person is not expected to express his feelings of anguish and loss. Death is not expected or permitted to cause any great disturbance in the usual flow of familial, vocational or social activities and expectations. This denies what modern psychological research and clinical psychiatric practice have established beyond doubt; namely, that the expression of grief is a necessary and thoroughly healthful pattern of reacting to bereavement. To inhibit or repress the normal expression of grief and anguish at the irreparable loss of a loved one can only result in the postponed release of the pent-up energies and impulses, usually in the form of neurotic symptoms. Open grieving at the time of the death, in the company of sympathetic relatives and friends, is the best antidote and preventive. This has been known and applied for thousands of years in Judaism.

The general desire to ignore the reality of death finds its counterpart in the attitude that is prevalent towards aging and the aged in contemporary American society. By and large, the elderly person in our society no longer commands a position of respect and worth. His very existence has become a problem to the younger generations.

Conversely, present-day American culture not only tends to shun the aged, but centers its greatest attention on youth. The scientific sophistication of modern, industrial society with its fantastic capacity to create abundance through mass-production, has placed great emphasis on the commodities that can be acquired to enhance the material comforts of living. Our materialistic values and the kind of activities spurred by our boundless appetites for creature comforts and financial success can flourish best in a youth-centered society. Americans are naturally inclined, therefore, to develop their life patterns and values around the youthful model. Consequently, the twilight years of life—so rich in wisdom and experience, but so far removed from the spirit of youthfulness—are ignored. Rejection of the aged may also be based partially on fear of death since the elderly person tends to symbolize death through his physical decline and degeneration. The patronizing tolerance or open repugnance felt for the aged in our society are thus seen to be motivated to a large degree by unwholesome forces. This attitude is far removed from the respect and deference paid to the aged in the traditional sociocultural system of Judaism, which taught: "Thou shalt rise in the presence of the aged." The decline of the influence of the aged and the attention given to the young both contribute to denial of the fact of death. The result is that people in our modern American society are removed from reality in this respect. If the inescapable fact of death can be tampered with and denied by large masses of the population, can the truths of the moral law be guaranteed survival for long? Does this not afford us some clues as to the possible origin of the widespread phenomena of delinquency and disruption so evident on the current scene?

Because of the tendency to ignore and deny aging and death in our society, there is no psychologically sound and generally accepted individual or social pattern for confronting death and bereavement and expressing grief in the majority culture. Laws and customs which have religious sanction and universal acceptance, such as were found traditionally in Judaism, are absent in modern society.

There is a disturbingly growing tendency in modern American Jewish life to ignore the reality of death and the basic needs of the bereaved and conform increasingly to the general attitude of the majority culture.

Modern American society has also turned the funeral into something "lovely" and unreal, conducted with soft music, perfumed flowers, honeyed circumlocutions, as "live" a corpse as the cosmetic arts can simulate, and a synthetic disguised burial. The whole purpose of the modern funeral is to mask the idea of death and the dead. The atmosphere of the funeral, totally unreal, must wind up being emotionally unsatisfying and psychologically frustrating. Instead of affording an opportunity to give vent to genuine feelings, to face the reality of death bravely, and to seek the support of others, it encourages all of the unwholesome mental mechanisms described earlier and fosters confusion and conflict. Its therapeutic value, therefore, is greatly diminished. Grief must be expressed in some way since the feelings engendered by bereavement are too strong to suppress. They may remain dormant for a while, but sooner or later they must come to the surface. The tensions and conflicts created by the death of a loved one can only be relieved through expression.

The absence of definite rituals and customs to guide the bereaved through the period of mourning, which comes after the funeral, is another serious lack in our American sociocultural system. In contemporary society there are no definite mourning patterns and few expectations of the mourner. He does not know what is expected of him, and consequently the therapeutic effect of the work of mourning is tragically lost. The unrelieved frustration of the love impulses toward the deceased and the intensification of feelings of guilt can create a situation where grief is distorted pathologically instead of assuaged, engendering ambiguity and confusion. Too much is left to the individual at a time when his helplessness and weakness are critical.

Our American culture does not meet the needs of the mourner. The threatened collapse of the traditional Jewish sociocultural system, depriving the Jew of the shelter of his self-contained Jewish community, would leave him just as bewildered in his grief as the non-Jew.

The various ethnic groups which first came to the United States brought with them their own sociocultural systems. With continual interaction among these groups, their unique ethnic systems gradually blended with each other and lost many of their indigenous characteristics. This is true of the Jewish culture as well as any other cultural group. The tendency to conform to the general pattern is great because each minority naturally identifies with the majority. The development of a definite, uniform pattern with respect to bereavement is hindered by the multiplicity and mobility of contemporary, middle-class society.

This may be why, with the process of assimilation still continuing, no definite American patterns have as yet emerged in regard to ritual observances for any of the critical phases of life, such as birth, puberty, marriage, and death. This general uncertainty affects all groups and all individuals during the period of widespread mobility.

Moreover, because of the very massiveness and concentration of the ethnically and religiously splintered American society, the experience of active and direct participation in the life of the community has become difficult to achieve. There is a multiplicity of organizations and institutions which attempts to answer the emotional needs of the people. But the variety of these organizations and their lack of a common cultural background increases the general confusion and uncertainty. The original modes of reaction to the crises of life tend to have lost much of their meaning in a society where many ethnic groups and sociocultural systems coalesce.

In this complex situation it may seem unrealistic and

naive to suggest the restoration of the rites and rules, the customs and the laws developed by the sociocultural system of Judaism, upon which the Jewish community thrived over the centuries and maintained a robust individual and communal existence. Yet this is exactly what the inescapable logic of our inquiry suggests.

We have already observed that Judaism developed effective therapeutic measures for the mourner. He was encouraged to relate to others, to face the reality of death and gradually to release the ties that bound him to the deceased. The efforts of each member of the Jewish community were directed to helping the mourner through his period of helplessness, giving him comfort and strength to face life again. With the dissolution of religious and communal life within Judaism, one of the most vital and proved systems of rehabilitation after the shock of bereavement would be lost to modern society.

Today, the synagogue has assumed the place of authority formerly held by the traditional laws and customs, which were woven into the very fabric of Jewish individual and communal life. Its authority may not be as effective as the sanctions of divine and human law, but the rabbis and leaders of the synagogue are still capable of conveying to the congregants to whom they minister the cogency and relevance of the observances developed through the course of Jewish history. The synagogue of today, furthermore, has one advantage over the institutions of the distant past. It can utilize the insights contributed by the behavioral sciences toward greater understanding of the human personality. These added insights can help to create new modes of handling bereavement, if necessary, in addition to adapting old ones.

One important way in which synagogal authority could be developed and implemented again would be through the establishment of a "Chevra Kadishah Committee" within each synagogue to function with respect to each bereavement in the congregation. Such a committee should be composed of volunteers, and could be of considerable help to the bereaved members. The primary function of the traditional Chevra Kadishah was to make all funeral and burial arrangements and take care of the needs of the berieved during the initial mourning period. The duties and definition of this group could be extended to meet modern circumstances. It would be called immediately upon the occurrence of a death and would hasten to the home of the deceased to offer preliminary comfort to the bereaved and take care of the funeral arrangements. In this, they would naturally coordinate with the rabbi of their synagogue, helping not only to make the individual's experience of death and grief a much more communal affair than it usually is at present, but also to center it in the synagogue instead of allowing it to be dispersed amorphously and impersonally in the secular community. Funerals might tend to take place more often in the synagogue than at present, giving them a religious rather than a secular funeral parlor aura.

Such Chevra Kadishah committees would be instructed by the rabbis as to the Jewish aspects of the understanding and handling of grief and by experts in the psychological sciences as to what is involved in the bereavement crisis and how the newer insights can be utilized to facilitate the grief work. As the importance of the contribution which such a committee can make is communicated to the membership of each synagogue, they will come to accept and rely upon it as an authoritative source of information and assistance. The Chevra Kadishah Committee could then guide mourners as to the rites and rules they should fulfill, the abstentions to be observed, and the duration of the various divisions of the mourning period. It could also furnish the mourners with the post-funeral meal and arrange private worship services in the home during the first week of mourning. It could also invite them to public worship in the synagogue during the year of mourning, to say "Kaddish" and to participate in the "Yizkor" (memorial) services.

Once authoritativeness is achieved by the Chevra Kadishah Committee, many of the traditional enactments and customs may become meaningful once again. For example, such committees could insist on keeping funerals simple and symbolic of the bereavement, arranging a dignified Mourner's Meal instead of a catered feast, assuring that a proper quorum will be present for services each evening at the mourner's home throughout the period of Shivah, reminding the family of the deceased about the obligation of reciting Kaddish in the synagogue every Friday evening or Saturday morning during Avelut and on every anniversary of the death.

The Jewish mourning laws and customs, although meaningful and therapeutic, cannot be imposed on the individual mourner. However, the Chevra Kadishah Committee can be effective in gaining acceptance from them once more, especially if the committee is composed of respected and sincere members of the congregation. These will be given the opportunity to gain a deep understanding of the complexities of grief and to share in developing a modern therapeutic system of grief work based upon traditionally hallowed and psychologically sound principles and procedures.

The problem of communicating the vital importance of re-establishing this old-new way of handling the grief situation should become the responsibility of the rabbi of every synagogue, and should likewise become a project of all the rabbinical associations in this country. In this way a great contribution can be made to the grief-stricken in the Jewish community, and perhaps ultimately in all the world.

A BIBLIOGRAPHY FOR "A TIME TO MOURN"
By Roberta Halporn, M.A.

Introduction

Rabbi Jack Spiro composed this fine commentary on Jewish funeral and bereavement practices in 1967, long before the current wave of death awareness swept America. Unavailable to him at that time were the literally hundreds of fine books which now compose an extensive literature of thanatology—the study of aging, death, dying and bereavement. What is remarkable about this second edition is that the flood of new literature which succeeded Rabbi Spiro's original text has not produced a single volume to substitute for it. This unusual circumstance points to at least two significant facts—first that Jewish funeral and memorial practices are informed by an eternal wisdom, and second, that Rabbi Spiro was perceptive enough to capture the essence of that wisdom and reveal it for the modern reader.

What is astonishing for the thanatology bibliographer is to discover that only a meager few publications can be added to update this source list that relate to Jewish customs. This testifies to the neglect by contemporary Jewish philosophical and religious theoreticians on an issue in which the American public has leaped far ahead. Though the majority of the pioneers in the death and dying field are themselves Jewish, the interpretation of Jewish customs and values for modern society has marched from the pens of mostly secular writers.

It is therefore even more vital that Rabbi Spiro's contribution be restored to distribution and Bloch Publishing Co. deserves a special commendation for perceiving this need and acting upon it.

Selected Bibliography

Books:

Agee, James. *A Death In The Family.* *1971*. New York: Bantam Books.

Aries, Phillipe. *The Hour of Our Death.* *1981*. Helen Weaver, Trans. New York: Alfred E. Knopf.

Bailey, Lloyd R., Sr. *Biblical Perspectives on Death.* *1979*. Philadelphia, Pa.: Fortress Press.

Beauchamp, Thomas, and Perlin, Seymour. *Ethnical Issues in Death and Dying 1978.* Englewood Cliffs, N.J.: Prentice-Hall.

Bendann, Effie. *Death Customs. An Analytical Study of Burial Rites.* *1971*. Detroit, Mich.: Gale Research Company.

Brown, Norman O. *Life Against Death.* *1959*. Boston, Mass.: Wesleyan University Press.

Carse, James. *Death and Existence.* *1980*. New York: John Wiley and Sons.

Eissler, Kurt R. *The Psychiatrist and the Dying Patient.* *1955*. New York: International Universities Press.

Frazer, James G. *The Fear of Death in Primitive Religion.* *1977*. New York: Ayer Press
———. *The Golden Bough. A Study in Magic and Religion.* *1983*. New York: The Modern Library

Freud, Sigmund. *The Basic Writings of Sigmund Freud. 1938.*
James Strachey, Trans. New York: The Modern Library
————. *Beyond the Pleasure Principle.* James Strachey, Trans.
1975. New York: W. W. Norton and Co.
————. *Civilization and Its Discontents.* James Strachey,
Trans. 1962. New York: W. W. Norton and Co.
————. *Group Psychology and the Analysis of Ego.* James
Strachey, Trans. 1975. New York: W. W. Norton and
Co.
————. *Inhibitions, Symptoms and Anxiety.* Alix Strachey,
Trans. 1977. New York: W. W. Norton and Co.
————. "Mourning and Melancholia," *Collected Papers.*
1956. Vol. IV, pp. 152–172. London: The Hogarth
Press.
Gorer, Geoffrey. "The Pornography of Death." *Death, Grief
and Mourning. 1971.* New York: Arno Press.
Heilbrunn, Gert. "On Weeping." *P.Q. 1955.* XXIV, 2.
pp. 245–255
Klein, Melanie. "Mourning and its Relation to Manic-De-
pressive States." Now found in: Peretz, David, *et al. Eds.
Death and Grief: Selected Readings for the Medical Student
1977.* New York: Health Sciences Publishing Corp.
Lindenmann, Erich. "Symptomatology and Management of
Acute Grief." Now found in: Carr, Arthur, Eds. *et. al.
Grief: Selected Readings. 1975.* New York: Health Sciences
Publishing Corp.

The Funeral:

Central Conference of American Rabbis. *Gates of Prayer. For
the House of Mourning, Afternoon and Evening Services. 1975.*

New York: C.C.A.R.

Consumer's Reports. *Funerals: Consumer's Last Rights.* 1977. New York: Random House.

Irion, Paul. *The Funeral. Vestige or Value.* 1971. Milwaukee, Wis: Bulfin Press

Mitford, Jessica. *The American Way of Death.* 1978. New York: Simon and Schuster.

Margolis, Otto. *Acute Grief. Counseling the Bereaved.* 1981. New York: Arno Press.

Morgan, Ernst. *Dealing Creatively with Death and Dying.* 1984 Burnsville, N.C.: Celo Press.

Pine, Vanderlyn R. *et al.* Eds. *Acute Grief and the Funeral.* 1976. Springfield, Ill.: C. C. Thomas Pubs.

Nelson, Thomas C. *It's Your Choice.* 1982. Washington, D.C.: A.A.R.P. United Synagogue of America. *A Plain Pine Box.* (Film) New York: United Synagogue of America.

Books for Children on Funerals and Loss:

Grollman, Rabbi Earl. *Talking About Death. A Dialogue Between Parent and Child.* 1974. Boston, Mass.: Beacon Press

Johnson, Marv and Joy. *Tell Me Papa. Tell Me About Death & Funerals.* 1978. Omaha, Neb.: Centering Corp.

Levy, Erin Lynn. *Children Are Not Paper Dolls* (For siblings). 1982, ———.

Pomerantz, Barbara. *Bubby, Me and Memories.* 1984. New York: Union of American Hebrew Congregations.

Spiro, Moshe Halevi. *Zaydeh,* 1984. Lawrence, N.Y.: Simcha Pub. Co.

About Children and Death:

Bowlby, John. *Loss. 1975.* Part III of *Attachment, Separation, and Loss. 1975.* New York: Basic Books.

Gordon, Audrey, and Klass, Dennis. *They Need to Know. How to Teach Children about Dying and Death. 1979.* Englewood Cliffs, N.J.: Prentice-Hall.

Grollman, Rabbi Earl. *Explaining Death to Children. 1974.* Boston, Mass.: Beacon Press.

Kubler-Ross, Elisabeth. *On Children and Death. 1983.* New York: The Macmillan Co.

Rudolph, Marguerite. *Should the Children Know: Encounters with Death in the Lives of Children. 1978.* New York: Schocken Books.

Schowalter, John, *et al.,* Eds. *The Child and Death. 1983.* New York: Columbia University Press.

Jewish Sources:

Central Conference of American Rabbis. *The Rabbi's Manual. 1961.* New York: C.C.A.R.

Epstein, I., Ed. *The Talmud. 1958.* London: The Soncino Press

Ganzfried, Solomon, Ed. *Code of Jewish Law. (Shulchan Aruch Chosam Mishpot)* Hyman E. Goldin. trans. *1963.* New York: Hebrew Publishing Co.

Freehof, Solomon. *Modern Reform Responsa. 1971.* New York: Ktav Publishing Co.

———. *Reform Jewish Practice. 1952.* New York: Ktav Publishing Co.

Friedman, H. and Simon, Maurice, Eds. *The Midrash Rabbah.* *1951.* London: The Soncino Press.

Ginzberg, Louis. *The Legends of the Jews.* Henrietta Szold trans. *1954.* Philadelphia, Pa.: The Jewish Publication Society of America.

Greenberg, Sidney, Ed. *A Treasury of Comfort.* *1954.* N. Hollywood, Cal. Wilshire Book Co.

Jastrow, Morris, Jr. "Dust, Earth and Ashes as Symbols of Mourning among the Ancient Hebrews." *J.A.O.S.* XX, pp. *133–150.*

———. "The Tearing of Garments as a Symbol of Mourning." *J.A.O.S.* XXI, pp. *23–39.*

Katz, Robert L. "Empathy in Modern Psychotherapy and in Aggada." *Hebrew Union College Annual.* *1959.* XXX. *191–215.*

Khayes, Kh. "Beliefs and Customs in Connection with Death." *1930. Yiddish Scientific Institute, Studies in Philology,* II, *281–328.*

Lamm, Rabbi Maurice. *The Jewish Way In Death and Mourning.* *1969.* New York: Jonathan David Pubs.

The Mishnah. Philip Blackman, trans. *1962.* New York: Judaica Press.

Noveck, Simon, Ed. *Judaism and Psychiatry.* *1956.* New York: The National Academy for Adult Jewish Studies of the United Synagogue of America.

Riemer, Rabbi Jack. *Jewish Reflections on Death.* *1974.* New York: Schocken Books, Inc.

Schauss, Hayyim. *The Lifetime of a Jew.* *1950.* New York: Union of the American Hebrew Congregations.

Sperka, Joshua S. *Eternal Life: A Digest of All Laws of Mourning.* *1939.* New York: Bloch Publishing Co.

Zborowski, Mark, and Herzog, Elizabeth. *Life is With People*
    1962. New York: Schocken Books.

Bereavement:

Gerber, Irwin, A. Weiner, and Kutscher, A. H., *et al.*,
    Eds. *Perspectives on Bereavement. 1979*. New York: Arno
    Press.
Jackson, Edgar N. *The Many Faces of Grief. 1982*. Nashville,
    Tn.: Abingdon Press.
Kushner, Harold S., *When Bad Things Happen to Good People.*
    1981. New York: Schocken Books.
Lewis, C.S. *A Grief Observed. 1961*. New York: Seabury
    Press.
Linzer, Rabbi Norman. *Understanding Bereavement. 1981.*
    New York: K'tav Publishing Co.
Moffat, Mary Jane, Ed. *In the Midst of Winter: The Literature*
    of Mourning. 1982. New York: Random House.
Montgomery, Herb and Mary. *Beyond Sorrow. Reflections on*
    Death and Grief. 1977. Minneapolis, Minn.: Winston
    Press.
Weir, Robert F., Ed. *Death in Literature. 1981*. New York:
    Columbia University Press.

All books listed, except those that are out of print, may be
obtained from the Center for Thanatology Research and
Education, Inc., 391 Atlantic Ave., Brooklyn, N.Y.
112117. A master bibliography of current titles is also
available in the fields of Aging, Dying and Death, upon
request.

Index

DATE DUE